Project-Based Learning

Project-Based Learning

How to Approach, Report, Present, and Learn from Course-Long Projects

Harm-Jan Steenhuis and Lawrence Rowland

BEP BUSINESS EXPERT PRESS

Project-Based Learning: How to Approach, Report, Present, and Learn from Course-Long Projects

First published in 2018 by
Business Expert Press, LLC
222 East 46th Street, New York, NY 10017
www.businessexpertpress.com

ISBN-13: 978-1-63157-475-7 (paperback)
ISBN-13: 978-1-63157-476-4 (e-book)

Business Expert Press Portfolio and Project Management Collection

Collection ISSN: 2156-8189 (print)
Collection ISSN: 2156-8200 (electronic)

Cover and interior design by Exeter Premedia Services Private Ltd., Chennai, India

First edition: 2018

10 9 8 7 6 5 4 3 2 1

Printed in the United States of America.

Abstract

Project-based learning is different from traditional lectures and requires students to behave different from the traditional classroom. This book provides students guidance on how to deal with the project-based instruction form.

Different types of projects such as projects that contribute to theory and projects that contribute to practice are covered, to explain to students what to expect, how to approach the project, how to interact with students in groups, and how to interact with the instructor. The discussion includes many useful examples.

Keywords

client report, effective presentations, experiential learning, groups, instructor feedback, iterative process, pedagogy, problem-based learning, professional report, project management, project-based learning, projects, research paper, service learning, teaching

Contents

CHAPTER 1

Problematic Higher Education

With the high cost of a college degree, it is not surprising that the question often asked is: Does it pay to go to college? Although studies have clearly established that there is an economic value of going to college, the reasons why college matters are complex. While, when looking at the time period from 1992 to 2012, young adults who did not attend college were approximately 2.5 times more likely to be unemployed than those who finished college, when recently looking at how college graduates do in the labor market, the results are disappointing (Arum and Roksa 2014). For instance, Arum and Roksa (2014) found that two years after graduation, over half of the graduates not re-enrolled full-time in school were either unemployed or underemployed, and for those that were employed, many of them were in low-paying jobs. Furthermore, 25 percent of college graduates were still living at home and parental support went considerably beyond simply providing a place to sleep and instead parents were covering many of their living expenses (Arum and Roksa 2014).

Arum and Roksa (2014) found that the performance on critical thinking, complex reasoning, and written communication (as measured by the Collegiate Learning Assessment (CLA) is significantly associated with the likelihood of experiencing unemployment. This means that graduates with low CLA scores might have greater difficulties with securing employment opportunities, and if employment was secured, then employers determined that these graduates were unable to perform at adequate levels, and thus, they lost their jobs (Arum and Roksa 2014).

Limited Student Learning

Arum and Roksa (2011) did an extensive study based on the CLA to measure student learning. The CLA was designed to assess core outcomes espoused by all of higher education: critical thinking, analytical reasoning, problem-solving, and writing. They found that students on average had little improvement from their freshman entrance to the end of their sophomore year. An average-scoring incoming freshman (50 percent) would reach a level equivalent to the 57th and 68th percentile of the incoming freshman class, respectively, toward the end of the sophomore year and senior year. In the 1990s and 1980s, the gains were much higher. Furthermore, at least 45 percent of the students did not make statistically significant gains in critical thinking, complex reasoning, and writing skills (Arum and Roksa 2011).[1]

The Role of Educational Preparation

There are several factors that contribute to Arum and Roksa's (2011) discouraging findings of limited improvement during undergraduate programs. For instance, the background of students when they enter college plays a role. Students in the top 10 percent of the sample improved their CLA performance considerably more. If these freshmen entered higher education at the 50th percentile, they would reach a level equivalent to the 93rd percentile of an incoming freshman class by the end of their sophomore year (Arum and Roksa 2011).

Another factor is parents' education. Students whose parents held graduate or professional degrees had a notable advantage over first generation students, that is, whose parents had no college experience (Arum and Roksa 2011).

Another contributing factor is the approach students take toward homework in college. Arum and Roksa found that students are not spending a great deal of time outside of the classroom on their coursework. On average, they report spending only 12 hours per week studying, and 37 percent of the students reported spending less than five hours

---

[1] Interestingly, despite limited gains on the objective CLA measure of critical thinking, complex reasoning, and writing, when students were asked how much they *believed* they had developed on their skills in these areas, students overall believed that they had substantially improved their skills in these areas (Arum and Roksa 2014, p. 38).

per week preparing for their courses (Arum and Roksa 2011). Only 20 percent of students reported devoting more than 20 hours per week on studying, whereas, in 1961, this was 67 percent (Arum and Roksa 2011). Despite the limited amount of time spent on studying, students seem to do well in terms of grades. On average, students were academically evaluated as relatively successful by the instructors of the courses they had chosen. The average collegiate grade point average of students was 3.2. Furthermore, national research has highlighted the extent to which grade inflation is rampant not only throughout higher education, but particularly at elite colleges and universities. For example, in 1997, the median GPA at Princeton was 3.42, and the proportion of course grades that were A or A-minuses was 45 percent at Duke, 44 percent at Dartmouth, and 46 percent at Harvard.

What happens in the classroom is of course also important. Lecturing remains the pre-eminent method of teaching (Ramsden 2003, p. 147). However, a drawback of the lecture is that it is often teacher-directed (Ramsden 2003). Research has shown that the traditional lecture mode of teaching is only effective for low-level factual material, often only dealing with factual recognition or recall (Gardiner 1994, p. 39) and where students typically employ surface, rather than deep approaches to learning (Ramsden 1994; Biggs 2003). Therefore, it has been observed that the lecture style, where students only devote minimal time to intellectual work yet with apparent ease pass through the American colleges and universities, is partly to blame for the poor performance of graduates (Gardiner 1994; Arum and Roksa 2011). Instead, approaches such as where students are active, work in teams, and apply material may be more effective (Michaelsen, Davidson, and Major 2014; Wallace et al. 2014). The overall feel for a class in that case is one about learning to do something, as opposed to learning some facts so that one can pass a test (Michaelsen, Davidson, and Major 2014).

The Setup of this Book

This book discusses an alternative approach to the lecture mode of instruction, that is, where students are active, work in teams, and apply material through project-based learning. Figure 1.1 illustrates the topics that are

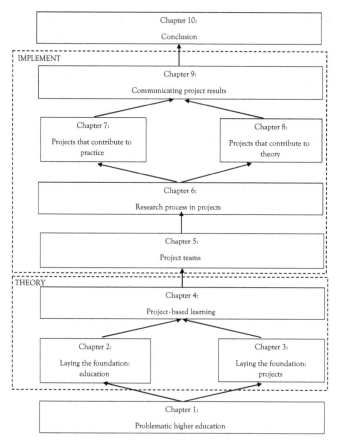

Figure 1.1 Topic coverage

covered in this book. The first three chapters lay the theoretical base for understanding project-based learning. Chapters 2 and 3 start by building the foundation. These chapters provide what can be considered background information, but this information is important to understand the context in which project-based learning takes place and why this approach is a better alternative than the lecture-based approach. Chapter 2 explains how education *works* and Chapter 3 provides information on projects. Chapter 4 combines aspects from education and projects and explains the concept of project-based learning. The next five chapters discuss the implementation of project-based learning. Classroom projects are typically conducted in groups; therefore, Chapter 5 discusses project teams. Chapter 6 describes some general characteristics related to the research component of projects and Chapters 7 and 8 discuss more details for two different types of projects, that is, those that contribute to practice and those that contribute to theory. While both types of projects have similarities, there are also some differences. These chapters also include advice on how to go about doing a project. Chapter 9 provides information on how to report on projects through writing as well as for presentations. Some information is already provided in Chapters 6 and 7 as examples, but Chapter 8 provides more clarification. Finally, the book ends with Chapter 10, which provides a conclusion on project-based learning.

CHAPTER 2

Laying the Foundation: Education

Chapter 1 demonstrated that university graduates have difficulty finding jobs, and that performance and improvement of university graduates on skills such as critical thinking, complex reasoning, and written communication are disappointing. A variety of reasons exist for these trends. One of the key factors that influences student learning relates to what happens in the classroom, and what happens in the classroom relates to pedagogy and the design of courses and programs. In order to understand and appreciate why the lecture-based approach does not always lead to the desired results, or why project-based learning is a better alternative, it is necessary to gain insight into how education works. Therefore, this chapter provides the foundation, or background, on education and learning. It starts with explaining Bloom's taxonomy. This is a frequently used tool to design programs and courses in terms of what students should be learning in those programs and courses. Next, the discussion moves to how students approach learning followed by a discussion on how instructors approach learning. Finally, some conclusions are drawn.

Educational Objectives and Bloom's Taxonomy

Educational goals and objectives are the *key building blocks* for any program, such as an MBA program, as well as for any individual course because they determine what students should get out of the program or course, that is, what they are supposed to learn. The international business school accreditation agency AACSB International—The Association to Advance Collegiate Schools of Business (AACSB)—views program learning goals as broad statements of accomplishment that cut across the curriculum.

Goals can be stated as "Upon graduation our students will…" and as such they state expectations that reflect the depth and breadth of student knowledge and skill. The goals express what students will be or have as a result of completing the program.

Learning *objectives* describe a measurable attribute of the overall learning goal. The objectives thus describe what educators want the students to do or make as evidence of achieving the objective. For each learning objective, an assessment device or process must be developed to allow an evaluation of student performance on that objective (AACSB International Accreditation Coordination Committee 2013).

In other words, educational programs have goals that get translated into objectives that are specific and measurable. These objectives get assessed by instructors and educators, so that they can determine whether students learned the knowledge and skills that they were supposed to learn. Needless to say, the formulation of learning objectives is, therefore, very important.

In 1948, the idea for a classification system of educational objectives was formed at the American Psychological Association Convention in Boston. Over the next years, a team of scientists under the leadership of Benjamin Bloom developed a taxonomy of educational goals. This taxonomy contained three domains: cognitive, affective, and psychomotor. The cognitive domain deals with the development of intellectual abilities and skills. The affective domain deals with changes in interest, attitudes, and values, and the development of appreciations and adequate adjustment. Last, the psychomotor domain relates to the manipulative or motor skill area (Bloom 1956). The emphasis in this book is on the cognitive domain.

The taxonomy for the cognitive domain was designed to be a classification of the student behaviors that represent the outcomes of the educational process (Bloom 1956, p. 12). The developed taxonomy led to six classes of student learning objectives, in hierarchical order from simple to complex: knowledge, comprehension, application, analysis, synthesis, and evaluation (Bloom 1956, p. 18), see Table 2.1. In other words, when a course or educational program is designed, instructors need to consider the complexity level in student learning. Learning can be at a simple level,

Table 2.1 Taxonomy of educational objectives

	Simple					Complex
The cognitive domain	1. Knowledge	2. Comprehension	3. Application	4. Analysis	5. Synthesis	6. Evaluation

Source: Adapted from Bloom et al. (1956).

Table 2.2 The taxonomy table

	The cognitive process dimension					
The knowledge dimension	1. Remember	2. Understand	3. Apply	4. Analyze	5. Evaluate	6. Create
A. Factual knowledge						
B. Conceptual knowledge						
C. Procedural knowledge						
D. Meta-cognitive knowledge						

Source: Adapted from Anderson et al. (2001).

such as learning knowledge, that is, memorization, but learning can also be more complex, such as for example, analysis, which is higher-order learning. For a student to be able to adequately analyze requires that the student already has mastered the underlying levels of knowledge, understanding, as well as the ability to apply.

In the 1990s, the handbook was revised and new knowledge about learning was incorporated into the framework. This led to an additional dimension, that is, the *knowledge dimension*, while the previous six classes of objectives were rearranged as *cognitive process dimensions*, see Table 2.2 (Anderson et al. 2001).

In this revised taxonomy, factual knowledge is knowledge of discrete, isolated content elements. Conceptual knowledge is knowledge of more complex, organized forms. Procedural knowledge is knowledge of how to do something, and metacognitive knowledge is knowledge about cognition in general, as well as awareness of and knowledge about one's own cognition (Anderson et al. 2001, p. 27).

In terms of the cognitive process dimension, remember relates to retrieving relevant knowledge from long-term memory. Understand relates to constructing meaning from instructional messages, including oral, written, and graphic communication. Apply relates to carrying out or using a procedure in a given situation. Analyze relates to breaking material into constituent parts and determining how parts relate to one another and to an overall structure or purpose. Evaluate relates to making judgments based on criteria and standards, and create relates to putting elements together to form a coherent or functional whole, reorganize elements into a new pattern or structure (Anderson et al. 2001, p. 31).

An important issue for educators is to be able to assess what students learned, and in this regard, Anderson et al. (2001, p. 67) further divided this cognitive process dimension into 19 cognitive processes that fit within these six categories, see Table 2.3. Based on Table 2.3, it is possible to formulate and distinguish 19 different educational objectives for student learning, and it also identifies how learning can be assessed. For example, in terms of analysis, a student should be able to distinguish relevant from irrelevant parts or important from unimportant parts of the presented material. Thus, on a test, a student could be presented with both relevant and irrelevant information and then be asked to demonstrate the ability to analyze.

With this taxonomy, it is also possible to explain the weaknesses of the traditional lecture format. The lecture approach is transmission- and teacher-oriented. This means that the teacher shares his or her information and the student then tries to remember this information. In other words, it is focused on the lowest-level cognitive process, whereas skills such as critical thinking, analytical reasoning, and problem-solving are associated with the higher, more complex cognitive levels.

Student Approaches Toward Learning

Although lecture-based learning is aimed at lower levels of learning, this does not mean that students cannot achieve higher levels of learning. Although course design in this situation does not provide much direction or incentive, it is nevertheless possible for students to achieve higher levels of learning with the lecture approach, but this depends upon the activities undertaken by the student and how the student approaches the work.

Table 2.3 The cognitive process dimension

Process dimension	Cognitive process	Definition	Example
Remember	Recognize or identify	Locating knowledge in long-term memory that is consistent with the presented material	Recognize the dates of important events in U.S. history
	Recall or retrieve	Retrieving relevant knowledge from long-term memory	Recall the dates of important events in U.S. history
Understand	Interpret or clarify, paraphrase, represent, translate	Changing from one form of representation to another	Paraphrase important speeches and documents
	Exemplify or illustrate, instantiate	Finding a specific example or illustration of a concept or principle	Give examples of various artistic painting styles
	Classify or categorize, subsume	Determining that something belongs to a category	Classify observed or described cases of mental disorders
	Summarize or abstracting, generalizing	Abstracting a general theme or major point	Write a short summary of the events portrayed on a videotape
	Inferring, or concluding, extrapolating, interpolating, predicting	Drawing a logical conclusion from the presented information	In learning a foreign language, infer grammatical principles from examples
	Comparing or contrasting, mapping, matching	Detecting correspondences between two ideas, objects, and the like	Compare historical events to contemporary situations
	Explaining or constructing models	Constructing a cause-and-effect model of a system	Explain the causes of important 18th century events in France
Apply	Execute or carrying out	Applying a procedure to a familiar task	Divide one whole number by another whole number, both with multiple digits
	Implementing or using	Applying a procedure to an unfamiliar task	Use Newton's second law in situations in which it is appropriate

(Continued)

Table 2.3 The cognitive process dimension (Continued)

Process dimension	Cognitive process	Definition	Example
Analyze	Differentiating or discriminating, distinguishing, focusing, selecting	Distinguishing relevant from irrelevant parts or important from unimportant parts of the presented material	Distinguish between relevant and irrelevant numbers in a mathematical word problem
	Organizing or finding coherence, integrating, outlining, parsing, structuring	Determining how elements fit or function within a structure	Structure evidence in a historical description into evidence for and against a particular historical explanation
	Attributing or deconstructing	Determine a point of view, bias, values, or intent underlying the presented material	Determine the point of view of the author of an essay in terms of his or her political perspective
Evaluate	Checking or coordinating, detecting, monitoring, testing	Detecting inconsistencies or fallacies within a process or product; determining whether a process or product has internal consistency; detecting the effectiveness of a procedure as it is being implemented	Determine whether a scientist's conclusions follow from observed data
	Critiquing or judging	Detecting inconsistencies between a product and external criteria, determining whether a product has external consistency; detecting the appropriateness of a procedure for a given problem	Judge which of two methods is the best way to solve a given problem
Create	Generating or hypothesizing	Coming up with alternative hypotheses based on criteria	Generate hypotheses to account for an observed phenomenon
	Planning or designing	Devising a procedure for accomplishing some task	Plan a research paper on a given historical topic
	Producing or constructing	Inventing a product	Build habitats for a specific purpose

Source: Adapted from Anderson et al. (2001, p. 67); Clark and Ernst (2010); Hanna (2007); Kratwohl (2002); and Pickard (2007).

Anderson et al. (2001) provide three learning scenarios, see Table 2.4. Table 2.4 illustrates how the approach that students take toward learning can influence the outcome of the learning process. With the lecture approach, many students will use rote learning, which can accomplish success in the lower process dimension *remember*. A student might also follow a more meaningful learning approach that, even in a lecture situation, can lead to higher-level learning such as *apply*.

A similar distinction is made by Biggs (2003). Biggs uses Figure 2.1 as an illustration. Biggs (2003) uses the example of two students who attend a lecture.

Susan is academically committed; she is bright, interested in her studies and wants to do well. She has clear academic or career plans, and what she learns is important to her. So when she learns, the goes about it in an "academic" way. She comes to the lecture with sound, relevant background knowledge and possibly some question she wants answering. In the lecture, she finds an answer to her preformed question; it forms the keystone for a particular arch of knowledge she is constructing. Or it may not be the answer she is looking for, and she speculates, wondering why it isn't. In either event, she reflects on the personal significance of what she is learning.

Robert is at the university not out of a driving curiosity about a particular subject or a burning ambition to excel in a particular profession, but to obtain a qualification for a decent job. He is not studying in the area of his first choice. He is less committed than Susan, possibly not as bright, academically speaking, and has a less developed background of relevant knowledge; he comes to the lecture with few questions. He wants only to put in sufficient effort to pass. Robert hears the lecturer say the same words as Susan heard, but he doesn't see a keystone, just another brick to be recorded in his lecture notes. He believes that if he can record enough of these bricks, and can remember them on cue, he'll keep out of trouble come exam time.

Students like Robert are in higher proportion in today's classes than was the case 20, even 10, years ago. The challenge instructors

Table 2.4 Three learning outcomes

Learning outcome	Learning approach
No learning	Student A reads a chapter on electrical circuits in her science textbook. She skims the material, sure that the test will be a breeze.
	When she is asked to recall part of the lesson, she is able to remember very few of the key terms and facts. For example, she cannot list the major components in an electrical circuit, even though they were described in the chapter.
	When she is asked to use the information to solve problems (as part of a transfer test), she cannot. For example, she cannot answer an essay question that asks her to diagnose a problem in an electrical circuit.
	In this worst-case scenario, student A has neither sufficiently attended to nor encoded the material during learning.
	The resulting outcome can be characterized as essentially no learning
Rote learning	Student B reads the same chapter on electrical circuits. She reads carefully, making sure she reads every word. She goes over the material and memorizes the key facts.
	When she is asked to recall the material, she can remember almost all of the important terms and facts in the lesson. Unlike student A, she is able to list the major components in an electrical circuit.
	When she is asked to use the information to solve problems, however, she cannot. Like student A, she cannot answer the essay question about the diagnosis of a problem in an electrical circuit.
	In this scenario, student B possesses relevant knowledge, but cannot use that knowledge to solve problems. She cannot transfer this knowledge to a new situation.
	Student B has attended to relevant information, but she has not understood it, and therefore cannot use it. The resulting learning outcome can be called rote learning.
Meaningful learning	Student C reads the same textbook chapter on electrical circuits. She reads carefully, trying to make sense out of it.
	When she is asked to recall the material, she, like student B, can remember almost all of the important terms and facts in the lesson.
	Furthermore, when she is asked to use the information to solve problems, she generates many possible solutions.
	In this scenario, not only does student C possess relevant knowledge, but she can also use that knowledge to solve problems and to understand new concepts. She can transfer her knowledge to new problems and new learning situations.
	Student C has attended to relevant information and has understood it. The resulting learning outcome can be called meaningful learning.

Source: Adapted from Anderson et al. (2001, p. 64) and Mayer (2002).

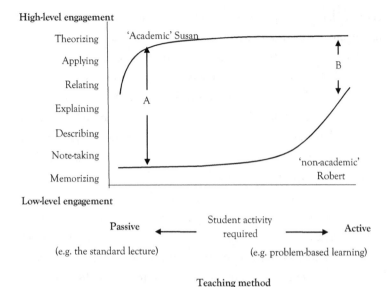

Figure 2.1 Student orientation, teaching method, and level of engagement

Source: Adapted from Biggs (2003, p. 4).

face is to teach so that Robert learns more in the manner of Susan. Figure 1.1 suggests that the present differences between Robert and Susan (point A) may be lessened by appropriate teaching (point B). This is influenced by the degree of learning-related activity that a teaching method is likely to stimulate (Biggs 2003, p. 3).

Biggs' (2003) characterization of Robert who is looking to do the minimum effort to pass the course is also aligned with the findings from Arum and Roksa who noted that the limited number of hours students spend studying is consistent with the emergence of a college student culture focused on social life and strategic management of work require-ments (Arum and Roksa 2011, p. 69). Related to this, Arum and Roksa (2011) posed two questions. How many times during the prior semester did students take a class where they wrote more than 20 pages over the course of the semester, and how many times did they take a class where they read more than 40 pages per week. About 50 percent of the students reported that they had not taken a single course during the prior semester that required more than 20 pages of writing, and one-third had not taken one that required even 40 pages of reading per week (Arum and Roksa 2011, p. 71). In other words, there is a combination of things going on that affects student learning in courses. The lecture-based approach aligns with, and entices students to use, a root learning approach, and aside from whether the students put in sufficient effort and adequate practices to learn the course material, they are also not required to do a lot of reading or writing. This relates to the left side of Figure 2.1.

Arum and Roksa (2011) conclude that, while, for instance, 99 percent of college faculty say that developing students' ability to think critically is a *very important* or *essential* goal of undergraduate education, and while 87 percent also claim that promoting students' ability to write effectively is *very important* or *essential*, the commitment to these skills appears more a matter of principle than practice (Arum and Roksa 2011, p. 35). To say it differently, while instructors may recognize the need to teach higher-order skills and knowledge, their approach to teaching may, nevertheless, be the lecture method, instead of the adoption of more active teaching methods. One reason for this may be the relative unimportance given to teaching. By 1989, faculty at four-year colleges overwhelmingly reported that scholarship was more important than teaching for tenure decisions in their departments. To the extent that teaching mattered in tenure decisions at all, student satisfaction with courses measured through student course evaluations was the primary measure that faculty considered relevant. This is a measure that partially encourages faculty to game the system by replacing rigorous and demanding classroom instruction with entertaining classroom activities, lower academic standards, and a generous distribution of high course marks. Research on course evaluations has convincingly demonstrated that higher grades do lead to better evaluations, and student course evaluations are not very good indicators of how much students have learned (Arum and Roksa 2011, p. 7).

These examples from Anderson et al. (2001), Biggs (2003), and Arum and Roksa (2011) show that how students approach learning and what activities they do affect the achievement of learning objectives. However, how students approach learning and what activities they do is influenced by how the course is designed, that is, what approach the instructor

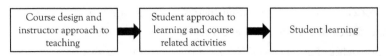

Figure 2.2 Relationship course design and student learning

follows. This is illustrated in Figure 2.2. Based on the examples, it also becomes clear that university professors may not be encouraged to deviate from the traditional lecture method of teaching, while a problem with this method is that it does not encourage students to develop the types of student behavior that encourages higher-level engagement. Consequently, the lecture can lead to a *surface approach* to learning. Biggs defines the surface approach as: arising from an intention to get the task out of the way with minimum trouble while appearing to meet course requirements. Low-cognitive-level activities are used when high-level activities are required to do the task properly. The concept of the surface approach may be applied to any area, not only to learning. The phrases *cutting corners* and *sweeping under the carpet* convey the idea: the job appears to have been done properly when it hasn't (Biggs 2003, p. 14). This contrasts with the *deep approach* that arises from a felt need to engage the task appropriately and meaningfully, so the student tries to use the most appropriate cognitive activities for handling it. When using a deep approach in handling a task, students have positive feelings: interest, a sense of importance, challenge, and even exhilaration. Learning is a pleasure. Students come with questions they want answered, and when the answers are unexpected, that is even better (Biggs 2003, p. 16).

Educator Approaches Toward Teaching

By now, it is clear that students have limited progress on skills such as critical thinking, analytical reasoning, and problem-solving. It has also been established that learning objectives can be divided into several different categories. This ranges from simple, such as memorization, to the more complex, such as hypothesizing. Furthermore, the achievement of learning objectives is dependent upon several variables, including the approach that students take to learning, and the approaches to learning are influenced by the teaching methods used. It was established that the most commonly used teaching method, that is, the lecture, is weak, in the sense that it does not encourage students to follow deep-learning approaches that align with higher-order learning. In this section, additional background is provided on approaches toward teaching to gain a deeper understanding of the classroom environment.

Two main paradigms of education have been recognized: the teaching-centered paradigm and the learning-centered paradigm (McManus 2001). The approach toward teaching has traditionally been a *teacher-oriented approach*. In this approach, the instructor is central, the instructor transfers information to students while students accumulate knowledge, and the assumption is that facts and concepts can be learned without experiencing or applying them (McManus 2001). This can be seen in the lecture method where the teacher just shares the information.

As noted by Arum and Roksa (2011, p. 131), "Scholarship on teaching and learning has burgeoned over the past several decades and has emphasized the importance of shifting attention from faculty teaching to student learning." In the *learning-centered approach,* the process of learning is as important as the content learned, the instructor creates a learning environment while students develop skills in constructing and using instructor's guidance, and an assumption is that facts and concepts must be tested and used to be learned (McManus 2001). The differences between teacher-oriented and learning-oriented are further illustrated by Samuelowics and Bain (2001), see Table 2.5.

Table 2.5 demonstrates, from an additional perspective, that teaching-centered orientations are weak in addressing higher-order learning because these orientations focus on simply sharing information and at best facilitating understanding. It is better to adopt learning-centered approaches, so that higher-order learning can be achieved. Learning-centered approaches focus on student activity and can be divided into two main theories: phenomenography and constructivism (Biggs 2003, p. 12). Phenomenography is based on the idea that the learner's perspective defines what is learned, not what the teacher intends should be learned. Teaching is a matter of changing the learner's perspective, the way the learner sees the world (Biggs 2003, p. 12). Constructivism is based on the idea that the learner has to construct their own knowledge

Table 2.5 *Different approaches to teaching*

Dimensions		Desired learning outcomes	Expected use of knowledge	Responsibility for organizing or transforming knowledge	Nature of knowledge
Teaching-centered orientations	Imparting information	Recall of atomized information	Within subject	Teacher	Externally constructed
	Transmitting structured knowledge	Reproductive understanding	Within subject for future use	Teacher	Externally constructed
	Providing and facilitating understanding	Reproductive understanding	Within subject for future use	Teacher shows how knowledge can be used	Externally constructed
	Helping students develop expertise	Change in ways of thinking	Interpretation of reality	Students and teacher	Personalized
Learning-centered orientations	Preventing misunderstandings	Change in ways of thinking	Interpretation of reality	Students	Personalized
	Negotiating understanding	Change in ways of thinking	Interpretation of reality	Students	Personalized
	Encouraging knowledge creation	Change in ways of thinking	Interpretation of reality	Students	Personalized

Source: Adapted from Samuelowics and Bain (2001).

(Mooney 2000, p. 61). They have in common the idea that what the learner has to do to create knowledge is important.

Conclusion

This chapter explained some of the background on educational processes and why or how students may graduate with or without certain skills. Essentially,

1. It was shown that there are different levels of cognitive processes such as those shown in the original and revised Bloom's taxonomy.
2. Instructors determine the student learning objectives for a course, and connected to this, have to determine what type of approach should be followed in the classroom.
3. When students follow courses at universities, they adopt approaches to learning and studying. The approaches that the students select are influenced by the approach that instructors follow toward designing their course.
4. Many students, as well as instructors, follow approaches that align with a lecture method. For students, this means that there are incentives to follow a rote learning approach.
5. While the lecture approach may be appropriate under certain circumstances, for instance, in lower-level courses where the emphasis is on establishing a knowledge base, educational programs also need to use classroom approaches that provide students with an opportunity to learn higher-order level learning skills.

It is recommended that students pay attention to the course and program learning objectives. This will create more awareness of what they are supposed to learn, as well as the level of learning. Furthermore, this can help them to determine the best studying approach to follow in individual courses.

CHAPTER 3

Laying the Foundation: Projects

There are several alternative approaches to the lecture-based method. These include the project-based learning approach. Before getting into the details of that specific approach (Chapter 4), in this chapter, some background information is provided on projects. Projects support a human need (Frame 2003). Evidences of early projects can be found in structures such as Stonehenge, the Egyptian pyramids, and the Great Wall of China. Construction of shelters, water systems, and roads are also examples of projects. The construction industry is one of the oldest project-based industries. Other traditionally heavily project-based industries include building and civil engineering, power, petrochemicals, pharmaceuticals, oil and gas, the extractive industries, shipbuilding, information systems and telecommunications, and defense/aerospace (Morris 1994). More than 80 percent of the organizations employing 100 or more workers utilize teams, including project teams (Chen, Donahue, and Klimoski 2004), and this number is considered by others to be an underestimation (Graen et al. 2006). So, projects are certainly not a new thing, and they form the basis for advancement around the world. Modern project management was born out of World War II and heavily influenced by Drucker's emphasis on management by objectives and process (Drucker 1974). This chapter provides foundational knowledge, or background, on projects from a general perspective. It starts by explaining the general context of projects. After this, types of uncertainties and what this means for a project environment are discussed. Next, and logically connected to this, is a discussion on how projects are approached, that is, their lifecycle. Then, the five basic processes are explained leading to a discussion of the basic processes for the different project lifecycles. Last, some conclusions are drawn.

Project Context

Managing projects in organizations can take on three separate scenarios: the project as a standalone project, a project within an organizational portfolio of projects, and a project within a larger program (PMI 2017a). All three scenarios assume some kind of overarching organizational strategy influencing and aligning the purpose of the projects, see Figure 3.1.

The organizational strategy is the set of objectives that provides direction in realizing the vision and mission of the organization. The vision "consists of two major components—a guiding philosophy that, in the context of expected future environments, leads to a tangible image" (Collins and Porras 2008). So, the values of the organization represented in the vision and mission get translated into proposed pathways to the future by the strategy. The actual pathways are the portfolios and programs that organize the benefits to be achieved.

Portfolios are "projects, programs, subsidiary portfolios, and operations managed as a group to achieve strategic objectives" (PMI 2017a, p. 714). Similar to a stock portfolio, project portfolios are ways for an organization to diversify and spread the risk in attainment of the objective. Portfolio projects are carefully selected to accommodate the available resources, respect the organizational and physical environment, and directly contribute to the strategic objective. Although portfolios are managed collectively for the benefit of the firm, the projects within

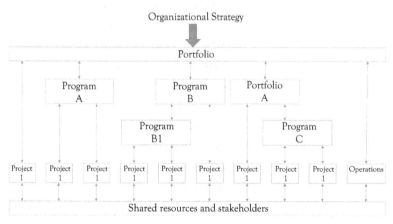

Figure 3.1 Portfolios, programs, projects, and operations

the portfolio have different purposes. For example, a construction firm may be erecting a new building in one project, refurbishing an office in another, and building out a retail store in a mall in a third project. All are construction projects, but they serve different owners and different objectives. Yet, they all fall under the strategic objective of the construction firm to service midsize commercial construction.

Programs are "related projects, subsidiary programs, and program activities that are managed in a coordinated manner to obtain benefits and control not available by managing program components individually" (PMI 2017a, p. 715). In keeping with the construction analogy, a large real estate development would be considered a program. Within the real estate development program, there would be various projects such as roads, utilities, buildings, landscaping, marketing, and financing, all contributing to one overall program objective, the successful development.

The common element here is that portfolios and programs are made up of projects. And, it is these projects that are the interface with the people who make it happen and the people who the project benefits. Projects are the grassroots of any organization that strive to meet a vision and mission through a strategy of portfolios and programs.

The next section reviews different environments in which projects may exist. These environments lead to different approaches or project lifecycles and account for the people, processes, and type of objectives one encounters in projects.

Project Environment

In the examples mentioned so far, the end products of the projects were tangible things such as buildings, bridges, or things such as computer data centers, or information technology networks. Increasingly, knowledge workers are being called upon to undertake projects that are less tangible and more complex, like software development (Schwaber 2009). What this shows is that projects take place in different types of environments. The Stacy Complexity Model, which has been adopted by project managers, is an insightful way of characterizing different project environments, see Figure 3.2 (PMI 2017b; Stacey 1996).

Figure 3.2 illustrates two characteristics of the project environment. First, one important characteristic is the methodological uncertainty. For example, for some projects, it may be clear how to approach it due to clear procedures that have proven successful in past projects, while not-done-before work may not have such clear procedures. The second characteristic is the requirements uncertainty. This relates to how much agreement there is on the requirements. For some projects, the bulk of the requirements may be known upfront and changes may occur through specific change request processes, while in other projects, the requirements may be a complex idea that has not been well articulated or defined thus creating uncertainties. The combination of these two characteristics leads to the characterization of a projects environment as either simple, complicated, complex, or chaotic.

A simple environment is the one in which there is some certainty in terms of methodology, as well as in terms of the requirements. A straight-forward homework assignment is a good example of a simple environment where there is certainty in terms of what needs to be done, as well as how it should be done. Complicated problems or environments add not only scale, but also requirements that include coordination and special skills (Allen 2016). A typical group project culminating in a document

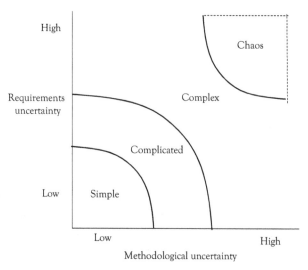

Figure 3.2 The project environment: uncertainty and complexity model (adapted from PMI 2017b)

and presentation is a good example of solving a prescribed complicated problem. The complex environment is probably better termed a complex system. Whereas, simple and complicated project environments have some predictable cause-and-effect relationships; these are not so apparent in a complex environment. The complex environment is more identified with stakeholder relationships, self-organization, and ongoing evolution (Allen 2016). Problems such as homelessness, poverty, and issues that transcend borders are good examples of complex systems. The most challenging project environments, that is, chaos, are those where there is a high degree of uncertainty for the methodology, as well as for the requirements. Although there are methods that can help guide a project team in chaotic situations, they are beyond the scope of this book.

Lifecycle Selection

The evolving project management landscape (Wysocki 2014) requires one to carefully consider and anticipate the appropriate project lifecycle for the project. The different environments have different management implications (Allen 2016). For example, a simple environment can be dealt with through step-by-step tasks that may involve new techniques or terminology that have a high chance of success if one follows directions (Allen 2016), but this approach is unlikely to lead to success in a complex environment. Understanding these environments, and being able to define a project's situation accordingly, provides insight into what type of project lifecycle approach is recommended, see Figure 3.3 (PMI 2017b).

Figure 3.3 illustrates what lifecycle approach best matches which type of project environment. The project life is defined by the following descriptions from the Agile Practice Guide (PMI 2017b).

- Predictive lifecycles take advantage of things that are known and proven. This reduced uncertainty and complexity allows teams to segment work into a sequence of predictable groupings. For example, an instructor may assign a paper that compares and contrasts two different articles. The process of reading, reviewing, analyzing, and documenting a response is simple and predictable. Other examples may include a

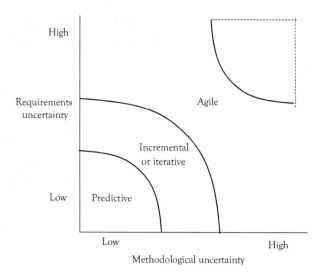

Figure 3.3 Project lifecycles under uncertainty (adapted from PMI 2017b)

simple construction project or event planning that requires a sequential step-by-step process to efficiently put all the pieces together for the final product or service. If one knows the steps and the timing involved, then for a project in its simplest form, a checklist could suffice to manage the project.

- Iterative lifecycles allow feedback on partially completed or unfinished work to improve and modify that work. For example, an instructor may assign periodic drafts of a major term paper prior to the submission of the final paper. In an ideal world, all students would embrace an iterative lifecycle for term projects where there is constant and consistent interaction with the instructor, rather than waiting until the last minute and doing it all one night with no opportunity to communicate and gain feedback from anyone.

- Incremental lifecycles provide finished deliverables that the customer may be able to use immediately. For example, even though they are not the finished products, the project management documents produced periodically throughout the project can be considered incremental deliverables. Or, more typically, what was planned as a full-featured software application may be introduced with increasingly more features or modules with successive versions. There is no reason to wait for the entire package to be finished when the customer can be satisfied earlier with something useful.

- Agile lifecycles leverage both the aspects of iterative and incremental characteristics. When teams use agile approaches, they iterate over the project to create finished deliverables. In keeping with the software application example, in an agile situation, the full slate of features may not be predetermined. The team gains early feedback and provides customer visibility, confidence, and control of the product, service, or solution. The iterations become incremental deliveries. Because the team can release earlier, the project may provide an earlier return on investment because the team delivers the highest value work first (PMI 2017b, p. 19). Remember, agile lifecycles are most appropriate for projects in complex environments. This requires more specialized expertise, increased communication, and feedback among stakeholders on a continuous basis.

Project Processes

Regardless of the type of project lifecycle as discussed in the previous section, a project lifecycle consists of basic processes. There is a widespread agreement that doing projects requires a lifecycle or a series of steps, phases, or processes (Alves et al. 2016; Bell 2010; Bilgin, Kemal, Karakuyu, and Eskisehir 2015; Larmer, Mergendoller, and Boss 2015; PMI 2017a; Trilling and Ginevri 2017). The challenge for all is agreeing on the number and names of the steps, phases, or processes. Here the five basic processes of the Project Management Institute (PMI 2017a) are adopted, that is, initiate, plan, execute, monitor and control, and close, see Figure 3.4.

Initiating represents "those processes performed to define a new project or a new phase of an existing project by obtaining authorization to start the project or phase" (PMI 2017a, p. 708). This is where the idea for a project and how it is achieved are articulated. The stakeholders are

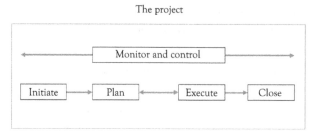

Figure 3.4 Project processes

identified, and their interests documented. The organizational strategy within which the proposed project will exist must align with the benefits proposed by the project. The initiating process is documented in the charter.

Planning takes initiating one step further and includes "those processes required to establish the scope of the project, refine the objectives, and define the course of action required to attain the objectives that the project was undertaken to achieve" (PMI 2017a, p. 713). Defining the course of action includes assigning roles and people to tasks, estimating task durations and cost, setting up processes to manage both risk and change, and anticipating project communications. This is all detailed in the project management plan document.

Executing includes "those processes performed to complete the work defined in the project management plan to satisfy the project requirements" (PMI 2017a, p. 706). This is where the work gets done. Most of the project's time and materials will be dedicated to the executing processes. All the planning will become real action during executing. As work is managed and completed, information is generated to define project performance.

Monitoring and controlling represents "those processes required to track, review, and regulate the progress and performance of the project; identify any areas in which changes to the plan are required; and initiate the corresponding changes" (PMI 2017a, p. 711). Monitoring and controlling extends across the entire project. The performance and consequences of the project are communicated through periodic status reports.

Closing processes are "performed to formally complete or close a project phase, or contract" (PMI 2017a, p 701). An important part of closing a project is lessons learned. Those lessons learned throughout the project are collected and reviewed by the team to assure continuous improvement.

Lifecycles and Process Groups

Integrating the four project lifecycles with the five basic project processes cycles as discussed earlier, leads to Figure 3.5. Although the same processes are used across the various lifecycles, their actual implementation may differ from one lifecycle to another. A key differentiator is the type of feedback that exists within the lifecycle.

For the predictive or linear lifecycle, the project follows a straightforward path from beginning to end. The low level of uncertainty involved allows for a step-by-step progression to the close of the project. The monitoring and control process provides the necessary feedback within the project to manage the project. Projects that have specific components can follow an incremental lifecycle. These components are preplanned and only need to be executed in the proper way to satisfy the project. When more uncertainty creeps in, the team must revisit the plan to assure the iterations are helping to realize the customer's need. The feedback extending back to the plan represents learning on the part of the team. The learning refines the plan for more effective execution. And, when the team is advancing into unplanned territories, they must look at planning

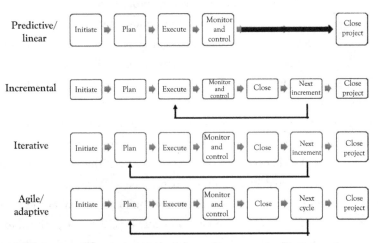

Figure 3.5 *Predictive, incremental, iterative, and agile lifecycles (adapted from PMI 2017b and Wysocki 2014)*

cycles to combine the incremental deliveries with iterative progress to the final product or service. Here, the feedback goes back to the plan and may represent an entirely new product to be executed based on what has been planned and done in previous cycles.

Conclusion

The purpose of this chapter was to understand projects broadly in preparation for working with projects to attain educational objectives. All projects exist within an organizational context, whether it is as a stand-alone project or part of a portfolio of projects and programs. This is significant in the alignment between the project and the organization's objectives. The projects that built our modern world have now embraced the increasing complexity of our modern times. Times are changing, and the contexts in which projects now exist are different than what they have been in the past. We now exist in a second machine age (Brynjolfsson and McAfee 2014). The production and economic rules have changed with digitization and massive computing power available to those with a computer. Approaches to projects are also maturing, as projects are increasingly involving more people in all organizations, and not just the traditional project-based organizations

The environment within which the project exists can be characterized by the level of uncertainty around the project requirements, that is, the objectives, and the methods to achieve these objectives. Appropriate project lifecycles exist for the four different types of project environments. While common basic processes occur across project lifecycles, the project lifecycles lead to difference in terms of, for example, the feedback loops. Project managers have to select an appropriate lifecycle for their environment. This is similar to selecting the right tool for a job. Applying the appropriate processes in the appropriate way to the appropriate lifecycle improves the chance of success for the project. The same applies to projects that are used in classroom environments. While one approach may be appropriate for one classroom environment, it may not lead to success in a different classroom environment. It is, therefore, critical for students to understand what the circumstances are in which their project is taking place.

CHAPTER 4

Project-Based Learning

Chapter 2 provided information on problems with the educational system. It explained how much of the university teaching is teaching-centered-oriented, that is, it involves lecturing, and how lecturing mainly addresses lower learning levels. It also explained how learning-centered-oriented approaches may provide a solution to the limited improvements that have been observed in student performance on critical thinking, analytical reasoning, problem-solving, and writing. A main distinction of these types of approaches is that they are oriented around student activities, that is, making the student an active participant instead of passive observer, and by doing that, deep learning is encouraged. Chapter 3 provided information on projects. Working on projects in a classroom setting is an example of an active learning approach and can be more effective than the lecture method. For example, "Students taught in small groups achieve higher grades, are more inclined to use a deep approach to learning, retain information longer and acquire greater teamwork and communication skills than students taught in the traditional manner" (Borg et al. 2011, p. 111), see also Oakley et al. (2004).

Like any skill, doing projects is something that requires orientation, preparation, practice, and a receptiveness to structure and guidance (Bairaktarova, Cox, and Srivastava 2015). Those students who show some kind of precommitment to project-based learning may be more effective in learning and retaining the efficacy of projects (Hao, Branch, and Jensen 2016). Student surveys indicate that it is only after going through a project or two that students begin to realize greater satisfaction, improved problem-solving skills, improved ability to integrate knowledge to find solutions, the promotion of their self-directed learning, and a preference for project-based learning over lectures and tutorials (Chua 2014). This chapter will provide additional information on projects in an educational context. First, it is explained how project-based learning is an active learning approach. This is followed by a discussion on types of projects. This has similarities to the discussion in Chapter 3 in terms of understanding the environment in which the project takes place. Then, an overview of classroom project environments is provided. The chapter ends with conclusions.

Active and Project-Based Learning

The difference between passive and active learning approaches is that, in the latter approach, students are actively involved in the learning process.[1] There are many different terms related to active forms of learning. This includes but is not limited to terms such as:

- active learning
- action learning
- anchored learning
- authentic learning
- case method
- design-based learning
- experiential learning
- inquiry-based learning
- problem-based learning
- project-based learning

---

[1] A similar notion is that of deductive versus inductive teaching, as identified by Prince and Felder (2006). In deductive teaching, for instance, engineering and science, "the instructor introduces a topic by lecturing on general principles, then uses the principles to derive mathematical models, shows illustrative applications of the models, gives students practice in similar derivations and applications in homework, and finally tests their ability to do the same sorts of things on exams. In inductive teaching, instead of beginning with general principles and eventually getting to applications, the instruction begins with specifics—a set of observations or experimental data to interpret, a case study to analyze, or a complex real-world problem to solve. As the students attempt to analyze the data or scenario and solve the problem, they generate a need for facts, rules, procedures, and guiding principles, at which point they are either presented with the needed information or helped to discover it for themselves" (Prince and Felder 2006, p. 123).

- service-learning
- simulation-based learning

These terms are not mutually exclusive, and the relationship between the different terms is not always clear and depends on the perspective taken.

For example, the Harvard Business School focuses on the use of the *case method*. In classroom discussion of cases, instructors use the Socratic method, in which students carry the discussion through answering to a stream of questions (Ellet 2007). The case method is described as:

> In a case method classroom, both the instructor and student must be active in different ways. Each is dependent on the other to bring about teaching and learning. Instructors are experts, but they rarely deliver their expertise directly. The art of a case method instructor is to ask the right question at the right time, provide feedback on answers, and sustain a discussion that opens up meaning of the case (Ellet 2007, p. 11).

In the case method, learners make the knowledge with the assistance of an expert and four types of situations occur in cases: problems, decisions, evaluations, and rules (Ellet 2007). Thus, from this perspective, problem-solving can be seen as a type of case method.

Another example is the use of the terms problem-based and project-based. In some instances, projects are considered types of problems. For instance, the Aalborg University in Denmark focuses on the use of problem-based learning. The problem is defined as being theoretical, practical, social, technical, symbolic-cultural, and scientific, and grows out of students' wondering within different disciplines and professional environments. The problem is the starting point directing the students' learning process, and it situates the learning in a context (Barge 2010, p. 7). From this perspective, cases and projects can be considered types of problem-solving (Stentoft et al. 2014). However, in other instances, solving problems can be considered part of a project.

In an attempt to come up with a meaningful distinction between problem-based and project-based, Stegeager, Thomassen, and Laursen

(2013) view problem-based as relating to the *orientation* of the learning process, that is, on problems, whereas project-based relates to the *organization* through which students address the problem and the main learning context of the students. While other views exist on how to distinguish problem-based from project-based learning, the assumption in this book is that the readers are not so much interested in the theories, and for ease of the discussion, problems will be considered a specific type of project.

What matters for the discussion is the general characteristics of problem-solving or project approaches that are used in classroom settings. These include the following (see e.g., Kolmos 1996; De Graaff and Kolmos 2003):

- They are student-centered and involve participant-directed learning processes or self-directed learning.
- It involves experience learning, that is, the student builds from his or her own experiences and interests.
- It involves activity-based learning. It requires activities involving research, decisionmaking, and writing.
- The instructor acts as a facilitator of learning, rather than as a transmitter of information. The facilitator (a) guides the development of higher-order thinking skills by encouraging students to justify their thinking and (b) externalizes self-reflection by directing appropriate questions to individuals (Hmelo-Silver 2004, p. 245).
- They have a problem orientation and are interdisciplinary. According to the dictionary, a problem could refer to a difficulty or even a riddle; in short, something you would want to get rid of as soon as possible. This is not the kind of problem that is meant here. A problem in project-based learning is an incentive for students, a challenge to start them off on their learning process; see de Graaff and Kolmos (2007).
- A central principle is that the student must gain a deeper understanding of the selected complex problem. However, there is an inherent risk with project-based learning that a sufficiently broad overview of the subject area is not provided. The students must, therefore, acquire the ability to transfer

knowledge, theory, and methods from previously learned areas to new ones.

- They take place in small groups, which means that the majority of the learning process takes place in groups or teams. Personal competencies are thereby developed so that students learn to handle the process of group co-operation in all of its stages.

Types of Projects

Classroom projects can be oriented on a variety of aspects and are organized around many characteristics such as the following:

- The *size* of the student team that works on the project. For example, projects can be conducted in small groups (3–5 students), but also larger groups (8–12 students).
- The degree of *complexity* of the project. This aspect is connected to the previous item of size as well as duration which is discussed below.
- Related to this complexity characteristic is the *level of Bloom's taxonomy* (Anderson et al. 2001) which is targeted in the project. Bloom's taxonomy was discussed in Chapter 2, where it was shown that this taxonomy has six levels. Two levels in particular play a role for projects. This relates to the "end objective" of the project.
  - Apply (level three): This involves using procedures to perform exercises or solve problems. An *exercise* is a task for which the student already knows the proper procedure to use. This is an example of a simple environment as shown in Figure 3.2. A *problem* is a task for which the student initially does not know what procedure to use, so the student must locate a procedure to solve the problem. This is an example of a complex environment as shown in Figure 3.2.
    - Executing (carrying out): This is applying a procedure to a familiar task (exercise).
    - Implementing (using): This is applying a procedure to an unfamiliar task (problem).

○ Create (level six): This involves putting elements together to form a coherent or functional whole; reorganize elements into a new pattern or structure. Although the categories of understand, apply, and analyze may involve detecting relationships among presented elements, create is different because it also involves the construction of an original product. The other categories involve working with a given set of elements that are part of a whole; on the other hand, in create, the student must draw upon elements from many sources and put them together into a novel structure or pattern relative to his or her own prior knowledge. The creative process can be broken into three phases: problem representation in which a student attempts to understand the task and generate possible solutions; solution planning, in which a student examines the possibilities and devises a workable plan; and solution execution, in which a student successfully carries out the plan.

  ▪ Generating (hypothesizing): This is coming up with alternative hypothesis based on criteria.

  ▪ Planning (designing): This is devising a procedure for accomplishing some task.

  ▪ Producing (constructing): This is inventing a product.

Two main dimensions are the *role* of knowledge, which relates to the learning orientation of the project and the type of *customer* for the final outcome of the project, which combined lead to four different types of project environments as illustrated in Table 4.1.

- The *role* of knowledge relates to what the students already know and how this plays a role in the project. On the one hand, a project may be used to teach the students the knowledge by having the students *discover* the theories for themselves. In other words, rather than passively listening to a lecture, the students use the project to actively search for knowledge. On the other hand, the students may already possess the knowledge and *utilize* this knowledge through

Table 4.1 Environment of classroom projects

Orientation of the project	Project orientation is to contribute to practice	*Developing an export plan before learning export theories*	*After having learned export theories, applying them by developing an export plan*
	Project orientation is to contribute to theory	*Trying to explain the known success of a global startup leading to studying born-globals and contributing to the theory on born-globals*	*After having studied theory on born-globals, identifying an industry in which this has not yet been studied or applied, and therefore doing a research project in that industry, which leads to new theoretical insight*
		Discovery The project directs the search for knowledge	*Utilization* The existing knowledge is applied in a project
		Role of theory or knowledge	

Source: The authors.

active application in a particular project. Another way of viewing this difference is that, on the one hand, the project is the central teaching strategy, that is, the students learn the central concepts of the discipline via the project, while on the other hand, the project serves as a type of assessment method, that is, the project is where students demonstrate what they have already learned through applying it in the project situation.[2]

• The type of *customer* relates to whether the project is mainly intended to contribute to practice or whether it is intended to contribute to theory. For example, in a consulting-oriented situation, the project is intended to help a client, and therefore is practice-oriented, while a paper for a scientific conference is intended to contribute to the scientific knowledge base, and is therefore theory-oriented. Note that, even though

---

[2] This is similar to but slightly different from Thomas (2000, p. 3) who distinguishes the project as a central teaching strategy versus situations where the project follows traditional instruction in such a way that the project serves to provide illustrations, examples, additional practice, or practical applications for material taught initially by other means. This also relates to the difference in deductive versus inductive teaching as identified by Prince and Felder (2006).

projects should be embedded in real-life situations, the project can have a real-life focus, as in a situation when there is a client, or it can be made up, that is, there is no real client. For example, the project could involve developing a strategy for a publicly known company without really working for the company. In that situation, the project would rely primarily on the availability of secondary data. Another example of a made-up project is a project that involves a simulated environment, for example, a business game. Another example of a made-up situation is anchored instruction.

In anchored instruction, the problem is a video-based story that presents learners with a challenge at the end such as determining if a certain school project can be profitable. The problem has two roles in anchored instruction. First, it provides an opportunity for learners to apply their shared knowledge to a relevant problem. Second, the video supports ongoing problem comprehension as problems often require 15–20 steps for solution (Hmelo-Silver 2004, p. 237).

Additional variables that define the context of the project are characteristics such as the duration of the project and the amount of guidance that is provided. Combinations of these aspects result in a large variety of projects as illustrated in Figure 4.1.

- *Duration* of the project. For example, small projects can be included in a single class session, while more complex projects may be semester long.
- *Instructor guidance* during the project. De Graaff and Kolmos (2007, p. 5) used the degree to which projects are self-directed, and based on this, they identified three types of projects.
  - The *task project* is characterized by a very high degree of planning and direction on the part of the teacher (teaching objectives) to the point where this most of all resembles a large task to be solved. Both the problem and the subject-oriented methods are chosen in advance, so that the students' primary concern is to complete the project

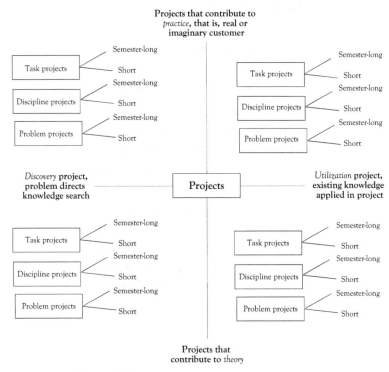

Figure 4.1 Types of classroom projects

according to the guidelines provided. Kolmos (1996) provides a metaphor for this type of project in terms of a football game. For the task project, the location of the field is known, the location of the ball is known, and the rules for play are known. Therefore, this is just a matter of playing the game. The task project has limited methodological uncertainty and also limited requirements uncertainty. It is representative of a simple environment, see Figure 3.2.

○ The *discipline project* is usually characterized by a rather high degree of direction from the teacher's side (study program requirements), in that the disciplines and subject area methods are chosen in advance. It may, however, still be dependent on the groups to identify and define the problem formulations within the guidelines of the described disciplines. These subject guidelines are described in the theme descriptions. Kolmos (1996) also provides a metaphor for the discipline project. For the discipline project, you know where the football field is and the basic football rules are also known, but before you can start to play, you have to find the ball.

o The *problem project* is a full-scale project for which the course of action is not planned in detail by the teachers. The problem formulation directs the choice of disciplines and subject area methods, and the problem formulation arises from the problem-oriented theme. De Graaff and Kolmos (2003) provide a metaphor. For the problem project, the students have the ball, but they do not know where the football field is nor do they have the playing rules. They have to start from scratch and set up the whole frame. The problem project has methodological and requirements uncertainties and provides a complex environment, see Figure 3.2.

Examples of Class Projects

In this book, the main focus will be on semester-long projects that are carried out by small groups (3–5 students in a group). To provide a little more insight into what the different types of projects are, and why these distinctions matter when conducting the class project, some examples will be provided as follows, and an overview is provided in Table 4.2.

Table 4.2 Example overview

Orientation of the project	Project orientation is to contribute to practice	Example C (problem project)	Example A (task project) Example B (problem project)
	Project orientation is to contribute to theory	Example D (discipline project)	
		Discovery The project directs the search for knowledge	Utilization The existing knowledge is applied in a project
		Role of theory or knowledge	

Source: The authors.

Chapters 5 through 8 will provide more details on managing the different types of projects, the communication of the project results, and so on.

Example A: Task Project with Utilization of Theory to Contribute to Practice

A representative from company X contacts the capstone course for help with developing a plan to export product Y to country Z. Teams of students work on this for the entire length of the academic term, that is, the semester. Students previously learned in other courses that were taken before they enrolled in the capstone course, to follow specific steps in the development of an export plan. The project is a matter of following these steps and filling in the information. Furthermore, the instructor has provided specific instructions on how to conduct this project and guides the students in the process, for example, giving instructions on how to write the export plan, what to include in the export plan, and where to find information.

This type of project is an example of a project that is in the top right of Figure 4.1 and Table 4.2 where the project contributes to practice, in this situation, with a real customer so that the project report, that is the export plan, would be written for and directed at company X. Students utilize knowledge that they already possess. It is also a semester-long project and a task project. This means that there is limited self-direction from students involved. Basically, what this means is that this type of project is not really student-centered (active learning), but instead it is teaching-centered where the problem and subject-oriented methods are chosen in advance. For the student, it resembles mostly a (large) task to be solved, and the primary concern is to complete the project according to the guidelines provided. This relates to lower-level learning in Bloom's taxonomy, that is, execute or implement.

The development of a similar export plan could also be a made-up situation if it does not involve a real customer, but if students use a made-up customer, for instance, an existing company where information can be found on the company website to help fill in the required information for the steps involved in the development of the export plan. In this situation, to add some realism to the situation, the project outcome, that is the project plan, should be directed at the existing company.

An example of a simulated project is one where (a small team of) students are led through a step-by-step simulation such as the first modules in the McGraw-Hill Practice Operations simulation. The first module in this simulation focuses on the basic production process in a make-to-order-oriented company that produces clothes. The production floor has three operations: cutting, sewing, and packaging. Orders come in and students get instruction on how to read the orders, and subsequently, on how to place commands in the simulated environment so that the clothes get produced. In the initial guided instruction, students are led from one screen to another where the settings of the simulation, the operations management content area, and the decisions that students have to make with the options that are available are explained. Students cannot deviate from this order. After the instruction, students have to play the simulation, but they still have limited self-direction. They cannot decide to tackle a different problem or use different methods. In this type of simulation, the face-to-face classroom and instructor are replaced by a computer screen, but other than that, it is a teaching-centered orientation where information is transmitted (through the simulation) to the student, who subsequently has a few options for decisions to experience different outcomes. Frequently, there are no reporting requirements in simulations because the student decisions can be viewed in the simulation data and results. Nevertheless, a course instructor could ask students to write a report, but in these instances, it usually involves some type of reflection upon the experience and the lessons learned.

Example B: Problem Project with Utilization of Theory to Contribute to Practice

In a capstone course, the instructor follows an anchored instruction approach. This means that the problem is a video-based story that presents learners with a challenge at the end. In this course, the students have to take on the role of consultants. The problem is that a bus manufacturer that has plants in Canada as well as in the United States is faced with a complex set of problems. This includes, but is not limited to: lack of orders, expected loss of approximately 30 percent of turnover, the bank has asked for the immediate payment of the full outstanding indebtedness, an engine supplier asks for a security position on future engine shipments, and of the employees who are union members, almost 90 percent voted in voted in favor of a strike. At the beginning of the course, the students have access to a video of the factory shopfloor, which explains the production process, and videos of interviews with key people inside the company, such as the owner of the company, CEO of the company, and Vice President Marketing. The students also receive a wide range of documents including information on the different buses, sales forecasts, actual sales, factory layout, production schedules, financial statements, and so on. Based on this information, the students have to come up with a solution, that is, advice for the owner of the bus company, such as, for example, a detailed plan for improvements or a sale of the company. This course project has a very high degree of student self-direction. Instructor guidance is limited and may only contain very broad directions to guide the process forward, such as guidance (an *assignment*) may be to advice the students to conduct an internal analysis without specifying the exact steps for doing this. After the completion of the assignment, the instructor may provide feedback, often in terms of asking additional questions, to provide further guidance. The project outcome, that is the plan, is directed at the owner of the company, or in other words, the made-up customer. More importantly, students are asked to reflect upon the process, their definition of the problem, their approach to solve the problem, the methods and tools they used to solve the problem, and so forth, and to reflect upon their learning.

This type of project is an example of a project that is in the top right of Figure 4.1 and Table 4.2 where the project contributes to practice, in this situation, with a made-up customer, so that the project report, that is the strategic plan, should be written for and directed at the owner of the company. Because of the nature of the capstone course, the students are already familiar with general business theories related to issues such as finance, marketing, and operations management. Therefore, in this situation, students have to utilize knowledge that they previously learned. A main difference with example A is that, in this example, there is limited guidance from the instructor; therefore, this is a problem project, rather than the task project from examples A and B.

Example C: Problem Project with Discovery of Theory to Contribute to Practice

A representative from company X contacts the introductory international management course for help with developing a plan to export product Y to country Z. Teams of students work on this for the entire length of the academic term, that is, the semester. As this is an introductory course on international management, students have not yet learned export theories. Therefore, at the beginning of the term, the students do not know how to approach the project, although they do have an assigned textbook that discusses export plans and how to develop them. Furthermore, the instructor does not provide specific instructions on how to conduct this project, but provides the students with guidance and advice on where to find information on how to go about developing an export plan. This means that the students do not have a specific set of instructions on how to approach this project. They, therefore, face a situation with a high degree of self-direction.

This type of project is an example of a project that is in the top left of Figure 4.1 and Table 4.2 where the project contributes to practice, in this situation, with a real customer, so that the project report, that is the export plan, would be written for and directed at company X. In this situation, the students have to search for and discover, that is, learn theories that explain how to develop an export plan. In this situation, they have to start by properly identifying the problem, which includes determining whether the company is even ready to export before blindly working on an export plan. Methods for analysis may include financial analysis, operations analysis, marketing analysis, and so on, which all have to be determined by the students as they progress through the project. The instructor provides feedback throughout the project in terms of advice on the results of analysis, where to find information, and so on. The project report is aimed at the company; therefore, the writing has to be aligned with this, which means, for example, practical advice, an operational plan with deadlines, responsibilities, and a financial plan to accompany it. This is a challenging situation to deal with as it includes higher-order learning. It also means that the students will reap different rewards in terms of what they learn compared with the previous examples A and B.

Example D: Discipline Project with Discovery of Theory to Contribute to Theory

In an international business course, an overall theme *developments in China* was established. Within this theme, the students were asked to do a research project where they had to contribute something new, that is, new knowledge. The initial orientation of the project was to develop a conference paper, that is, follow conference guidelines, although in the course, the projects were not actually submitted to a conference. The students did not have prior knowledge on developments in China. Based on an initial exploration, a student team found that, due to the previously adopted one-child policy, China was facing an aging population. Furthermore, the group also found that entrepreneurship may be linked to age. Therefore, they decided to increase their knowledge by studying the existing theory on aging population related to entrepreneurship within the context of China. Instructor guidance was limited, but contained broad directions to keep the scope of the project limited and to guide the project forward in terms of rough process steps such as to formulate a research purpose and research questions, to do a literature review, to develop a methodology, and so on. The instructor provided feedback and guidance on the process, which helped the students to move forward.

This type of project is an example of a project that is in the bottom left of Figure 4.1 and Table 4.2 where the project contributes to theory, but where the students have to discover the existing theory before they can determine a meaningful theoretical contribution. The project did not have a specific customer, and the projects results were, therefore, communicated broadly, but following scientific writing principles and aimed at an academic audience. This type of research project is very iterative in nature, and thus requires frequent adjustments by the students in their aim and scope of the project, which often come about through discussions with the instructor or facilitator on project progress.

Conclusion

In addition to the passive and teacher-centered lecture approach to teaching, there are several active and student-centered approaches. One of those approaches is the project-based learning approach. In the project-based learning approach, projects are used as an educational tool. An advantage of this type of approach is that the students gain more hands-on experience, and through following more deep-level learning approaches, will gain and retain the information better.

There are many different ways in which projects can be embedded into course design, and as a consequence, there are many different types of projects. Things such as the size of the student team, the length of the project, and the complexity all have an influence on the classroom project environment. Two key variables were identified. First, whether the project is oriented on contributing to theory or practice. Second, whether the project starts from existing student knowledge or whether the project is used to develop the student knowledge. Based on this, four different types of projects were identified. Furthermore, another important characteristic is the amount of guidance provided in the project. This was identified through three distinct approaches: task, discipline, and problem.

Projects can be very challenging for students, especially in situations where they have to discover the theory as this is quite different than what is experienced in lecture situations, and especially in problem situations where the guidance from the instructor is limited. Once a project has been introduced into a classroom situation, students should carefully consider what type of project environment they are facing, what this means in terms of the expectations in the course, and their approach to complete it successfully.

CHAPTER 5

Project Teams

In the previous chapters, the theoretical base for project-based learning was established. This is the first of several chapters, with more emphasis on the implementation of projects in classroom situations. Projects, including educational projects, typically involve groups of people. However, a collection or group of people isn't necessarily a team. For instance, when thinking in terms of a football or soccer team, what comes to mind is a group of people who are well-coordinated, guided by common goals, with an established leadership structure, and where team members know and have agreed upon their roles within the overall team. This isn't something that just happens, but something that gets developed over time. It is the same in educational situations, and students will not automatically function as a team and develop team skills simply by participating in groups (Salas et al. 2005; Baker 2008; Edmondson 2012).

Much research has been done on how collections of individuals develop into well-functioning teams over time. The Tuckman model provides an example (Tuckman 1965). Tuckman found that teams go through four stages:

1. A *forming* phase. Group members are initially concerned with orientation, which is accomplished primarily through testing. This testing serves to identify the boundaries of both interpersonal and task behaviors.
2. A *storming* phase. Group members display behaviors that serve as resistance to group influence and task requirements. This phase is characterized by conflict and polarization around interpersonal issues and related to this emotional responding in the task sphere.
3. A *norming* phase. In this phase, the resistance is overcome and in-group feeling and cohesiveness develop.

4. A *performing* phase. Finally, the group attains the last phase in which structural issues have been resolved. Roles become flexible and functional, and group energy is directed toward completing the task.

Another example is the team performance model that has been developed and refined over time by Drexler and Sibbet (Drexler, Sibbet, and Forrester 1988; Forrester and Drexler 1999; Sibbet 2002). This model contains seven stages that lead to a well-performing team:

1. An *orientation* stage. During this stage, the team members are dealing with the uncertainty of what the team is about, that is, why they are in the team. This stage is resolved once the team has, for instance, identified its purpose and when individuals have identified how they fit in the team.
2. A *trust-building* stage. During this stage, the team members are dealing with getting to know others in the team and determining what is expected of them. Developing trust is something that takes time.
3. A *goal clarification* stage during which there is discussion about what the team will be doing. This requires dialogue and understanding of roles, and so on. It often also requires debate to get clarity, and conflict is expected.
4. The *commitment* stage is a key stage in the forming of teams. During the three previous stages, the emphasis is on creating a team. In the last three phases, the emphasis is on sustaining the team and performing. The commitment stage is where the team takes the turn. A key issue is for the team to move into action. Sometimes, it requires going back to stage three for more clarification.
5. An *implementation* stage. Implementation requires that the team schedules and sequences activities and solves problems that arise. Tasks must be integrated and coordinated. Progress tracking is another important activity in this stage.
6. A *high-performance* stage. During this stage, the team is working in a state of synergy, flexibility, and intuitive communication. The high-performance stage is not stable, but experienced teams can do it more frequently. Issues such as overload and disharmony can arise.

7. The last stage is the *renewal*. This is when teams finish projects or, for example, experience changes such as taking on new members. Teams that are good at renewal take their time to realign with the original vision and goals and reconfirm the core values.

Others have identified similar stages (e.g., Graen, Hui, and Taylor 2006) and how team-level dimensions such as confidence, cooperation, coordination, cohesion, and conflict relate to well-performing teams (Capsim 2015). What is clear from these models is that teams get formed over time, and that conflict is a part of this process. The remainder of this chapter discusses three of the common elements in the team development models: forming of a group, dividing the work, and dealing with conflict.

Forming a Group

In a course, when groups get formed to work on a project, the forming of the group can be considered as being critical (Michaelsen, Davidson, and Major 2014). There are two key issues. First, how many students will be in a team? Second, who decides which students will be in which team? There is no consensus in the academic literature on either of these two issues, that is, it is not clear what an ideal team size is, nor the composition of the team, nor is there consensus on who should decide on who is in a team. Some of this may depend upon the environment or specific task that the team is working on (Stewart 2006). For instance, the project can be complex versus more routine; see also Chapters 3 and 4.

Project teams in classes can be of different sizes. Oakley et al. (2004) propose that groups are formed of three to four students, but Michaelsen, Davidson, and Major (2014) recommend teams of five to seven students. An advantage of smaller teams is that individual team members can't hide, and therefore, it is less likely that a team member is passive (Oakley et al. 2004). An advantage of larger team sizes, on the other hand, is that it is likely that it has better resources to perform the task. For example, the total skill set and time provided by the combination of team members (Stewart 2006).

Group composition is a related issue where some authors have argued for heterogeneity, while others recommend more homogeneity. Teams that have a heterogeneous composition, for example, diverse international backgrounds, offer advantages because they bring different things to the team. However, it may be better to select people based on different ability levels and personality traits, rather than member characteristics (Stewart 2006). An advantage of heterogeneity in terms of ability is that this provides weak students with good modeling of effective learning approaches and perhaps tutoring from strong students (Oakley et al. 2004). On the other hand, Borg et al. (2011) argue that homogeneous groups are preferred. For example, have teams composed of students with similar levels of ambition, as this leads to less conflicts. In this regard, they also recommend that friends aren't necessarily the best to have in a team. Oakley et al. (2004) also suggest that having friends on a team isn't necessarily good. They find that a tightly knit group of friends is more likely to incline toward covering for one another, rather than informing on infractions such as plagiarism or failure to participate in group efforts. On the other hand, Michaelsen, Davidson, and Major (2014) recommend that teams should be formed that minimize potential disruptions from cohesive subgroups such as pre-existing friendships. Baldwin, Bedell, and Johnson (1997) found that existing social networks mattered to important educational outcomes, including student satisfaction and team performance. Furthermore, while it might be expected that, in terms of performance, the team heterogeneity, or some forms of team heterogeneity such as international background or field of study, might be beneficial for creative work, and while it may be expected that homogeneous team composition might be better matched with more routine tasks, this has not been established in the academic literature (Stewart 2006).

Another issue is who decides which students are going to be in a team. One approach is that the instructor assigns students to a team. An alternative is that students select their own teams. A related aspect is whether teams have opportunities to change the group composition, for example, removing a team member who is perceived as not contributing (Borg et al. 2011; Oakley et al. 2004). There are pros and cons to each of these approaches, and there is no consensus in the scientific literature on which is better. For example, Borg et al. (2011) find that it might be best to let students choose their own group. This provides a possibility to avoid certain tensions as students, if they know each other from before, tend to choose group members with similar levels of ambition. Oakley et al. (2004), on the other hand, argue that instructors should form teams, rather than allowing students to self-select. One of their arguments is that this will prevent the stronger students to form groups and leaving the weaker students to form their own groups, which are likely to reinforce one another's misperceptions. Note, however, that, even if strong students form into groups, there is "no guarantee that teams composed of individuals selected for high individual performance will perform better as collective units" (Stewart 2006, p. 32).

All in all, the preceding discussion shows that there is little consensus on the best approach to the forming of teams in classroom project situations. Furthermore, there is no consensus on how the performance of teams relates to team characteristics, such as size and composition. What this practically means for students is that different instructors may use different approaches in their courses, and that students should be ready to deal with different situations. For instance, in some courses, there may be larger student-selected teams, while in other courses, there may be smaller instructor-selected teams. In some courses, teams may be heterogeneous, while in other courses, more homogeneous, and so on.

In all of these situations, in the early stages of a project team, the team has to be formed, and part of that has to do with getting to know each other and learning to trust (Salas et al. 2005). To aid group forming, it is recommended that people share information, such as topics shown in Tables 5.1, 5.2, 5.3, and 5.4, which may be collected and shared with instructors and other students.

Dividing the Work

Differences in what a team does and how a team uses the division of labor have been recognized. For example, Cohen and Bailey (1997) identified four types of teams, that is, work teams, parallel teams, project teams, and management teams. What matters in these teams, similar to the classroom situation, is how teams divide up the work. For example, project teams draw their members from different disciplines and functional units, so that specialized expertise can be applied to the project at hand (Cohen and Bailey 1997). Similarly, in a class project, students often divide the

Table 5.1 Getting to know you categories (adapted from Oakley et al. (2004))

Getting to Know You	
(If you feel uncomfortable answering any of these questions, you may leave that area blank. However, please complete as much as possible.)	
Name	
What would you like to be called?	
Address	
E-mail	Grades/GPA
Phone number (w)	Phone (h)
(optional) gender	
(optional) Ethnicity	
Academic major	
Year of study	
If returning for second degree, what was first degree in?	
Do you have a job aside from being a student? If so, what?	
What profession do you want to have and why?	
What is something about you that is probably not true of other students in the class?	
Favorite movie	
Favorite music or book	
Favorite hobby or sports activity	
What is the most beautiful sight you have ever seen?	

tasks into smaller pieces where everybody is responsible for their own piece, see Figure 5.1.

For example, when a team consisting of five students has to do an industry analysis by, for instance, applying Porter's five forces model, frequently the approach that is followed is where each person on the team conducts the analysis for one of the forces. When combined, this means that the entire model is applied and the industry is analyzed. However, when student teams break complex projects into separate elements in this manner, that is, with individual students focusing on their single element, then this is often to the detriment of more holistic understanding (Eliot et al. 2012). In this situation, a student may learn about and apply a small portion of the five-force model, but will not necessarily have understood the other four forces in the model. It is also likely that the overall analysis

Table 5.2 Getting to know you, adopted from Oaksley et al. (2004)

Getting to Know You

Times available for group work. In the following spaces, please cross out the times when you will NOT be available to work outside class assignments with your group. Mark only genuine conflicts, such as with classes or job responsibilities

Time	M	T	W	Th	F	Sat	Sun
8–9am							
9–10							
10–11							
11–12							
12–1pm							
1–2							
2–3							
3–4							
4–5							
5–6							
6–7							
7–8							
8–9							
9–10							
10–?							

Table 5.3 *Team policies, adopted from Oaksley et al. (2004)*

	Team Policies
	Your team will have a number of responsibilities as it completes problem and project assignments
1	*Designate a coordinator, recorder, and checker for each assignment. Add a monitor for a four-person teams.* Rotate these roles for every assignment.
2	*Agree on a common meeting time and what each member should have done before the meeting* (readings, taking the first cut at some or all of the assigned work, and so on.).
3	*Do the required individual preparation.*
4	*Coordinator checks with other team members before the meeting to remind them of when and where they will meet and what they are supposed to do.*
5	Meet and work. The *coordinator* keeps everyone on task and makes sure everyone is involved, the *recorder* prepares the final solution to be turned in, the *monitor* checks to make sure everyone understands both the solution and strategy used to get it, and the *checker* double-checks it before it is handed in. Agree on next meeting time and roles for next assignment. For teams of three, the same person should cover the monitor and checker roles.
6	*The checker turns in the assignment, with the names on it of every team member who participated actively in completing it.* If the checker anticipates a problem getting to class on time on the due date of the assignment, it is his or her responsibility to make sure someone turns it in.
7	*Review returned assignments.* Make sure everyone understands why points were lost and how to correct *errors.*
8	Consult with your instructor if a conflict arises that can't be worked through by the team.
9	Dealing with noncooperative team members. If a team member refuses to cooperate on an assignment, his or her name should not be included on the completed work. If the problem persists, the team should meet with the instructor so that the problem can be resolved, if possible. If the problem still continues, the cooperating team members may notify the uncooperative member in writing that he or she is in danger of being fired, sending a copy of the memo to the instructor. If there is no subsequent improvement, they should notify the individual in writing (copy to the instructor) that he or she is no longer with the team. The fired student should meet with his or her instructor to discuss options. Similarly, students who are consistently doing all the work for their team may issue a warning memo that they will quit unless they start getting cooperation, and a second memo quitting the team if the cooperation is not forthcoming. Students who get fired or quit must either find another team willing to add them as a member or get zeroes for the remaining assignments.
	As you will find out, group work isn't always easy—team members sometimes cannot prepare for or attend group sessions because of other responsibilities, and conflicts often result from differing skill levels and work ethics. When teams work and communicate well, however, the benefits are more than compensate for the difficulties. One way to improve the chances that a team will work well is to agree beforehand on what everyone in the team expects from everyone else. Reaching this understanding is the goal of the assignment on the *team expectations agreement* handout.

Table 5.4 Team expectations agreement, adopted from Oaksley et al. (2004)

Team Expectations Agreement
On a single sheet of paper, put your names and list the rules and expectations you agree as a team to adopt. You can deal with any or all aspects of your responsibilities outlined—preparation for and attendance of group meetings, making sure everyone understands all the solutions, communicating frankly but with respect when conflicts arise, and so on. Each team member should sign the sheet, indicating acceptance of these expectations and intention to fulfill them. Turn one copy in to the professor, and keep a remaining copy, or copies for yourselves.
These expectations are for your use and benefit; they are not graded or commented on unless you specifically ask for comments. Note, however, that, if you make the list fairly thorough without being unrealistic, you'll be giving yourselves the best chance. For example, "We will each solve every problem in every assignment completely before we get together" or "We will get 100 on every assignment" or "We will never miss a meeting" are probably unrealistic, but "We will try to set up the problems individually before meeting" and "We will make sure that anyone who misses a meeting for good cause gets caught up on the work" are realistic.

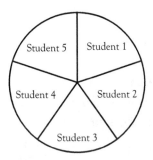

Figure 5.1 Each student does their own and equal part of the total

is simply attaching the separate analysis for each of the forces together without an overall understanding or reflection upon the entire model. This can also be obvious to an instructor or client of the project when not enough care is taken to align writing styles, formatting, and so on. In this instance, while team-level learning may have occurred, this doesn't always indicate learning at the individual level (Ellington and Dierdorff 2014). In situations such as these, if there is an exam in addition to the class project to assess whether students know and understand the material, there is a high likelihood that students will fail.

As the goal in education is often that all students learn all aspects and also because the ability to synthesize results is an important higher-level

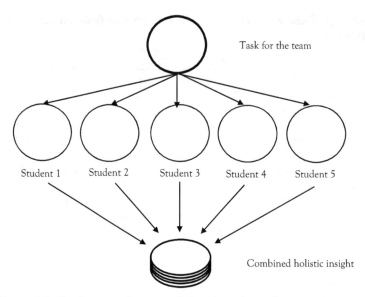

Figure 5.2 Students work in parallel and combine their insights

learning ability, see Bloom's taxonomy discussion in Chapter 2; a better approach for students is to work in parallel. That means, each student applies the entire model and draws his or her own conclusions. Then, in a team meeting, the different viewpoints can be shared, and based on this, conclusions are drawn by the entire team for the application of the entire model; see Figure 5.2.

This approach has clear learning advantages as not only will individual team members learn more about the model and its application, there is also an opportunity for weaker students to learn from stronger students in the team on how to improve their approach. This is one of the benefits of teamwork in a class context (McCorkle et al. 1999). No matter what approach is followed, teams need to communicate about their results, and it is recommended to use programs, such as PBworks, Google Docs, or learning management systems, such as Blackboard or Canvas, to share and jointly work on documents.

Conflict and Communication

One of the key features of student projects compared with the traditional lecture method of teaching is that, in project teams, there is interaction among students (Baldwin, Bedell, and Johnson 1997). As previously shown, this interaction can be quite beneficial from a learning perspective. It is also useful for students because organizations are increasingly seeking candidates who possess high levels of teamwork knowledge, skills, and abilities (Chen, Donahue, and Klimoski 2004). However, students often voice their frustration over cooperative structures, such as team projects (Baldwin, Bedell, and Johnson 1997), and sometimes perceive it as less-effective and efficient as lecture-based methods (Haidet, Kubitz, and McCormack 2014). Part of the reason for this frustration is that team projects are accompanied by conflicts. There are three types of conflicts in projects (Borg et al. 2011). First, there is conflict about how to fairly assign grades. Second, there are interpersonal conflicts that arise when students are expected to work together. Third, there is conflict about the time commitments and free riding. This last aspect is frequently encountered (see, for example, McCorkle et al. 1999; Stewart 2006) and appears to be especially an issue when projects require much more than usual investments by team members (Graen, Hui, and Taylor 2006).

As can be seen from the second stage, in the Tuckman model, that is storming (Tuckman 1965) as well as the second and third stage of the Drexler and Sibbet team performance model, conflict is *expected* when a collection of individuals change into a team. Conflicts are inevitable as groups mature, and conflicts are a natural part of group development (Kozlowski and Ilgen 2006; Borg et al. 2011). Dealing with conflict is, therefore, a part of the process of becoming a team, and a responsibility of a project team is to make sure that the conflict becomes productive and useful (Borg et al. 2011). This also means not simply agreeing with each other to agree (Ellis et al. 2003). Dysfunctional groups are *not* groups that experience conflict, but rather groups that are unable to deal with conflict and get stuck in the conflict stage (Borg et al. 2011).

Group projects give students an opportunity to develop the ability to overcome conflict. Avoiding, resisting, or not fully engaging in group work in order to avoid conflict is, therefore, doing a disservice to students (Borg et al. 2011). Students learn a lot from overcoming conflict. They learn how to work collaboratively and improve their communication skills. Students will be better prepared for their future work as professionals if they have learned how to handle conflict. This is regardless of the type of conflict, such as relationship or task conflict, and regardless of the satisfaction or team performance (De Dreu and Weingart 2003).

A key for dealing with conflict and team performance is communication (Baldwin Bedell and Johnson 1997). Communication alone is the most important indicator for team performance (Pentland 2012). Pentland (2012) identified three aspects of communication that affect team performance: energy, engagement, and exploration.

Energy relates to the number and nature of exchanges between team members. The most valuable form of communication is face-to-face. Pentland (2012) found that 35 percent of the variation in a team's performance is accounted for by the number of face-to-face exchanges. Phone conversations or video conferences are the next valuable form, but the more people participate, the less effective these forms of communication become. E-mail and texting are the least valuable form of communication.

Engagement reflects the distribution of energy among team members. If all members of a team have equal and relatively high energy with all other team members, then engagement is very strong. Teams where some members are engaged in high-energy communication, while others don't participate perform less.

Exploration relates to communication that team members engage in outside the team. It is essentially between a team and others or other teams. Higher-performing teams engage in more outside connections. However, exploration and engagement don't easily coexist because they require that the energy of the team is put to two different uses.

Communication is also related to the type of project environment and approach that was discussed in Chapter 3. Figure 5.3 illustrates the need for communication based on the complexity of the environment.

Tips for Making It Work

There are several suggestions for making the team work effectively. Some tips are provided as follows. Instructors may implement some of these techniques in the classroom. Even if instructors do not explicitly use some of these techniques, it is recommend for students to implement some of these suggestions, as it can help them from being a collection of individuals to becoming a well-functioning team.

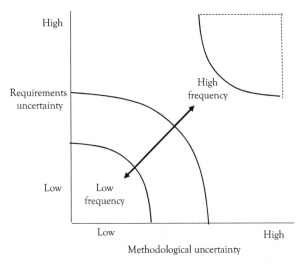

Figure 5.3 Communication need for project environment, adapted from PMI (2017b)

Pentland (2012) provides the following five points of advice in terms of team communication:

1. Everyone in the team talks and listens in roughly equal measure, keeping contributions short and sweet.
2. Members face one another, and their conversations and gestures are energetic.
3. Members connect directly with one another, not just with the team leader.
4. Members carry on back-channel or side conversations within the team.
5. Members periodically break, go exploring outside the team, and bring information back.

In terms of conflict, a good start to avoid team conflict is to have student teams prepare and sign a list of ground rules that everyone agrees to follow and to have well-defined roles (Borg et al. 2011). Examples include a team policies statement and team expectations agreement (Oakley et al. 2004) as shared earlier in this chapter. Rules can include coming to team sessions prepared, to outline problem solutions individually before the group meetings, and to communicate time conflicts (Borg et al. 2011). Some examples of these rules are provided in Appendix A. If conflicts escalate, then strategies such as *active listening* can help (Borg et al. 2011).

Another recommendation is to use peer evaluation (Oakley et al. 2004; Baker 2008; Lee and Lim 2014). Peer evaluation can help with non-formers in a group (Baker 2008; Borg et al. 2011; Lee and Lim 2014). For example, Baker (2008) found increased satisfaction with group work when peer assessment was used to reward those who made a greater contribution to group performance. Furthermore, instructors typically evaluate the quality of the final product without knowledge of the team work process, but peer evaluations can provide a tool to monitor the dynamics within the group (Lee and Lim 2012). Oakley et al. (2004) identify two alternative approaches to using peer ratings. One is to have students assess the *relative contributions* of the team members to the final product, usually expressing them as percentages of the total effort. The second approach is to have team members assess the *team citizenship* of each team member, such as cooperating with the team, fulfilling responsibilities, and helping others when possible. Baker (2008) provides an example for a peer assessment, see Table 5.5. Students can also design their own peer evaluation forms. This encourages thinking about what is most important for the team. Examples are provided in Appendix A. Peer evaluations can include or exclude self-rating. Self-ratings can bias the overall peer evaluation, but especially in small groups, it can be beneficial to include self-ratings. For example, if a group consists of three people and uses the team citizenship approach where two team members use relatively harsh peer ratings while one team member uses relatively lenient peer ratings, then, when looking at overall scores, the more lenient team member is going to have lower peer evaluation scores. This is because the more lenient team member will receive two harsh peer ratings, while the other two team members each have one harsh and one lenient peer rating. In a situation like this, it may be more fair and useful to include self-ratings.

Peer evaluations can be simply turned into the instructor without further distribution. This may provide input for grading. However, an important component of peer evaluation is to share feedback so that team members have an opportunity to learn and improve their ability to work in teams. This relates to the conflict that occurs when groups of

Table 5.5 **Example of a peer evaluation form**

	Student 1	Student 2	Student 3	Student 4
Preparation: Prepared for team meetings; has read course material and understands the issues and subject matter; completes team assignments on time; attends and is on time to team meetings.				
Participation and communication: Articulates ideas effectively when speaking or writing; submits papers without grammatical errors; listens to others; encourages others to talk; persuasive when appropriate.				
Helps group excel: Expresses great in interest in group success by evaluating ideas and suggestions; initiates problem-solving; influences and encourages others to set high standards; doesn't accept just any idea, but looks for the best ideas; stays motivated from the beginning to end of projects.				
Team player (cooperation): Knows when to be a leader and a follower; keeps an open mind; compromises when appropriate; can take criticism; respects others.				

This assessment uses a four-point scale (4 = usually (over 90 percent of the time); 3 = frequently (more often than not); 2 = sometimes (less than half the time); 1 = rarely (never or once in a great while)).

Source: Adapted from Baker (2008).

individuals transform into well-functioning teams because people may have different ideas about what constitutes good performance and acceptable or good behavior. Therefore, it is recommended to share feedback with team members. Thus, group members can share their evaluations with other group members so that these can be discussed in the group. This can enhance the formation of the team. An alternative that provides some anonymity in providing the feedback is the use of established programs such as Capsim's TeamMATE. This allows an assessment on individual-level dimensions such as preparation (analyzing and planning activities that enable performance), execution (collaboration and accomplishing team tasks), monitoring (assessing and evaluating ongoing performance), and adjustment (adapting and generating performance improvements), and how these affect the team-level performance in terms of confidence, cooperation, coordination, cohesion, and conflict (Capsim 2015). Based on peer evaluation, TeamMATE provides guidance to teams on how to improve.

Conclusion

After having established the foundation, that is, theoretical base, for project-based learning in the previous chapters, this chapter has focused on implementation of classroom projects. One part of classroom projects is to turn a group of individuals into a well-functioning team. This chapter has shown that there is limited consensus in the academic literature on how teams should be formed, the size of teams, and, for example, the composition of teams, that is, heterogeneous or homogeneous. What this means is, similar to working on project teams in organizations, that students have to be ready for and will experience a variety of project teams in different classroom environments. This gives students an opportunity to reflect on and learn from the differences that they experience. For example, they can compare how a team formed of friends with similar ambition can reduce conflict in the formation of teams compared to a team formed from students from a variety of backgrounds, but also experience how this can influence team performance.

It was also discussed that in many classroom projects, students divide up work so that each takes care of a small part of the whole. While in organizations, this may be beneficial as teams are composed of members with expertise in certain areas; this same approach has severe disadvantages in classroom situations, especially for discovery-oriented projects, see Chapter 4. This is because, with this approach, students may learn small parts, but will not sufficiently learn the whole or lack a holistic perspective. Therefore, it is recommended to work in parallel, that is, students each individually work on the task. They then meet to discuss their findings, and based on this, derive their conclusions. This reflection is one of the most important for learning.

Lastly, it was explained that conflicts are a natural part of the team formation process. While people may have a tendency to try to avoid conflict, and while many students have negative views because of the conflict that they experience in group projects, it is, nevertheless, beneficial to learn to deal with conflict and learn that it is a natural part of the team formation process. Several common types of conflicts exist, including the free rider or social loafing situation. Several recommendations were provided to effectively deal with the conflict situation, such as utilizing team contracts that spell out expectations and peer evaluations, which can also be used for grading purposes.

CHAPTER 6

The Research Process in Projects

Chapter 4 provided a classification of classroom projects. No matter what type of project is followed, in most instances, it will include doing research. Verschuren and Doorewaard (1999) observed the following about a research project:

> Carrying out a research project is a complex and lengthy activity. You are bombarded by a host of new impressions. Also, the various parties involved make different and often contradictory demands on you. In such a situation, many of you will find it hard to develop a goal-directed mode of action in which it is clear to yourself and to other parties involved what is going to happen. Still, the research project needs to incorporate a coherent body of activities, resulting in meaningful and sound insights. An important secondary objective is learning to work on a relatively extensive project according to a plan (Verschuren and Doorewaard 1999, p. 15).

As lower levels of education, such as primary and secondary education, place different demands on students in terms of the research aspect of projects, there is often a misunderstanding of the requirements for the research aspect in projects at the undergraduate or graduate university level. In particular, as research skills get developed over time, at lower levels of education, the emphasis is often on the *search* part. This means that students are used to doing research that consists mostly of finding and compiling information. However, for undergraduate and graduate projects, the research aspect needs to go beyond this skill set of searching and finding.[1] Instead, it has more emphasis on thinking critically about the data that was collected, the reliability of this data, and what conclusions can be drawn. The expected outcome of graduate-level research projects is generally something *new*, not simply a regurgitation of what is already known by compiling what others have done. This something new can, for example, be the development of a marketing plan for a client. While using existing theories and models, the situation is analyzed, and based on an application of existing models and theories something new, that is, the marketing plan is created. This chapter discusses four general characteristics of the research aspect of projects that are common across different types of classroom projects such as projects that contribute to practice (which will be covered more in-depth in Chapter 7) and projects that contribute to theory (which will be covered more in-depth in Chapter 8). The four general characteristics are: emphasis on critical thinking, different approaches, the iterative nature, and the danger of mission creep.

Critical Thinking

In general, the purpose of a project is to gain new insight, that is, something that did not exist before. This is the *outcome* of the project. However, in a classroom project, a more important purpose is typically for students to learn the research aspect that is a major component of the project process and to practice critical learning skills. That is, the skills necessary to be able to come up with something new and the ability to demonstrate that it is new. This requires a deep understanding of the variables, how they are measured, and the ability to draw conclusions and determine what this means and what type of research is necessary to improve the overall understanding, that is, what can be done that is new. This is the *process*

---

[1] See also Daniel (2013, p. 119) who explains this distinction. Furthermore, Daniel (2013) provides valuable recommendation on how to conduct research for projects in business situations. He identifies nine steps: identifying the area for the project, determining the topic of the research question, developing a tentative source list (with useful forms for tracking purposes), a working source list, making notes, developing the thesis that is the answer to the question, developing a skeleton plan, then a final plan, and then the writing.

of conducting the research aspect of the project. While an MBA is not a research-oriented degree, the practice of the critical thinking skills related to such projects is, nevertheless, critical for managers.

> Example: With the rise of the Internet, many people have been shopping online. And, apparently, this has had an impact on retail stores. Consider headlines such as "The Retail Bubble Has Now Burst: A Record 8,640 Stores Are Closing In 2017"[2] and "Department Stores, Once Anchors at Malls, Become Millstones."[3] With these types of headlines, it is easy to assume that retail is no longer viable, and that e-commerce is one of the main reasons for retail's fate. For example, in "5 Reasons Borders Went Out of Business (and What Will Take Its Place)," two particular reasons related to this and the bookstore's demise are that it was late with e-books and late to the Web, and furthermore that people are increasingly turning to digital books.[4]
>
> However, compare these headlines to the following headline "Amazon to Open Retail Store in Manhattan at Time Warner Center,"[5] which indicates that apparently the leadership of the online retailer Amazon considers retail as a viable business expansion! Other similar headlines also have appeared such as: "Online Retailers Moving Into Offline Shopping—Fast."[6] If someone was to believe these headlines, it seems that retail is very much an opportunity, and online stores are moving away from their traditional online business models and are opening up more brick-and-mortar stores.

---

[2] http://zerohedge.com/news/2017-04-22/retail-bubble-has-now-burst-record-8640-stores-are-closing-2017

[3] https://nytimes.com/2017/01/05/business/department-stores-macys-sears.html

[4] 5 Reasons Borders Went Out of Business (and What Will Take Its Place)

[5] https://nytimes.com/2017/01/05/technology/amazon-to-open-retail-store-in-manhattan-at-time-warner-center.html?mcubz=1

[6] https://forbes.com/sites/wendyliebmann/2013/05/30/online-goes-offline-fast/#89b788141d88

Suppose you are the manager of a retail store; what are you supposed to believe and do? If retail can no longer survive, it might be best to develop an exit strategy and limit the losses. But, if retail instead is alive and well, it might be best to develop a growth strategy. This is where the critical thinking skills from a project come in because if the research is properly conducted, then the application of critical thinking leads to the identification of the key underlying variables that are able to explain both phenomenon and that allows the development of, for instance, a strategic plan for a retail store. For instance, maybe retail is alive and well under certain conditions such as perhaps the types of goods that are sold, whereas under different conditions, maybe retail is doomed.

The research aspect of a project that is focused on the retail sector can, therefore, be relevant for projects that contribute to practice as well as projects that contribute to theory. New, useful, and powerful insights can especially be gained by examining situations where conflicting findings occur, such as the described situation of the retail sector. Another example of such a situation is that of outsourcing and reshoring. While some studies claim that (international) outsourcing is beneficial for companies (Trent and Monczka 2003), other studies show that outsourcing is more expensive than typically anticipated (Platts and Song 2010) and companies reshore their manufacturing (Benstead, Stevenson, and Hendry 2017).

In classroom projects that focus on contributing to theory, it is explicit that students have to search for theories, models, and so on, but students often underestimate how the same process has to be followed in projects that contribute to practice. The examples aforementioned on retail and outsourcing demonstrate that, unless a thorough understanding of the situation exists, it will be impossible to provide legitimate advice to a company.

The critical thinking skills that are practiced in the research aspect of a classroom research project are related to the higher-level learning skills in Bloom's taxonomy; see Chapter 2: analysis, evaluate, and create. The project is an excellent teaching method to develop critical thinking skills because, as indicated by Verschuren and Doorewaard (1999), different parts of the project make different demands on a student. The remainder of this chapter will cover themes that relate to the research during a project: research approach, iterative nature, and mission creep.

Types of Research Approaches

When looking at the research aspect, it is informative to look at the main approaches that occur in the context of business research. Another word for these approaches is paradigms, that is, a set of assumptions about the world and how, related to this, research should be conducted.[7] In the following, three approaches will be discussed that have traditions in the natural sciences, social sciences, and design sciences.[8] Business research falls within these different approaches.

Natural Sciences Approach

The first approach has its roots in the natural sciences such as physics, chemistry, and biology. The viewpoint here is that an apprehendable reality exists that is driven by immutable natural laws and mechanisms. The researcher and research object are considered independent of each other. This means that the researcher can, and should, objectively measure phenomena and not interfere with the data. Logically aligned with this, the preferred methodological choice is one of experimentation, manipulation,

---

[7] In the research methods literature, the discussion on paradigms relates to three elements: ontology, epistemology, and methodology (Denzin and Lincoln 1994, p. 99). Ontology deals with the nature of reality, epistemology deals with the relationship between the researcher and research object, and methodology deals with how we gain knowledge about the world.

[8] A fourth approach is that of the formal sciences. Formal or analytical sciences, such as mathematics, are primarily concerned with logical reasoning. They are not necessarily looking at empirical findings, but provided with a set of premises, a conclusion is derived, which logically must hold true. This *conclusion* can sometimes be tested as a hypothesis although this doesn't necessarily occur. There are also situations in which empirical tests are not (yet) possible. In business studies, this approach can be found in the area of management science or operations research. Simulations are sometimes added for the *testing* of the developed theories or models.

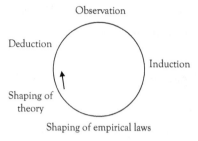

Observation

Deduction

Induction

Shaping of
theory

Shaping of empirical laws

Figure 6.1 Empirical cycle (adapted from de Groot (1969))

and the testing of hypothesis. Experiments, that is, repeating, can lead to generalizable results.[9] Related to this, an important concept in scientific research studies is the empirical cycle; see Figure 6.1.

The empirical cycle shows the sequencing of scientific research projects and is particularly relevant for projects that contribute to theory; see Chapters 4 and 8. In the natural sciences type of approach, the start is with the shaping of theory. This means, based on what is already known from previous studies, a new idea gets deduced or generated. This typically happens through the formulation of hypothesis. Next, data is collected to test or verify these hypothesis. Data collection in business research projects can occur through observation, but is often done through the use of surveys. Note that the underlying assumptions with the surveys are that the researcher is independent from the respondent and that there are limited interpretation issues of questions, which are normally worked out by testing a survey. Furthermore, all respondents get the exact same *stimulus*, that is, the survey, so that all data collected is comparable. Note that, in the case of interview surveys, the same rule applies, that is, each respondent has to receive the same stimulus, that is, questions, which are carefully designed in an interview script (Fowler and Mangione 1990; Fowler 2009). In a situation where respondents ask for clarifications, there might be specific strategies, that is, answers, in the interview script and interviewers should not deviate from the script. A main concern is that all respondents get the same treatment so that biases due to different

---

[9] This approach is known as the positivist- or post-positivist-oriented approach, see for example, Guba and Lincoln (1994).

treatments are avoided. Once unbiased data are collected, then based on the data, conclusions are drawn that lead to generalizations based on statistics, that is, statistical generalizations.

Key concerns in terms of evaluating this research approach are that the survey questions measure the variables in which the researcher is interested, that is, construct validity, and that the study can be repeated, and that this would lead to the same results, that is, reliability.[10] This approach is commonly known as the scientific method, but as will be shown next, it isn't the only approach to science or projects that contribute to theory.

Social Sciences Approach

Another approach, which is also particularly relevant for projects that contribute to theory, see Chapters 4 and 8, has its roots in the social sciences. The main difference with the natural sciences approach relates to the view on the relationship of the reviewer and the research object. The stance here is one where the researcher and the observed are not considered separate (Schwandt 1994, p. 125) because there is an interaction with humans. Furthermore, in order to understand the world of meaning, one has to interpret it, which means that it has subjective elements.[11] For these research approaches, it is essential that the *story* is being told so that the correct interpretations can be made. This type of research is, therefore, more concerned with reaching an in-depth understanding of particular cases. This means that researchers provide rich descriptions, and based on this, they make theoretical generalizations instead of statistical generalizations.

In terms of Figure 6.1, this approach has a different starting point. It is often more discovery-oriented instead of verification or testing. It starts with observation, then inductive thinking is applied to come up

---

[10] How one evaluates a research project is dependent on the paradigm. There are four generally accepted criteria for this (post) positivist research approach: internal validity, external validity, construct validity, and reliability.

[11] There are several paradigms related to this overall approach, but they contain differences. For example, an interpretivist still believes in a set of natural laws, although these have to be derived at through the interpretation of data, but a constructivist does not believe in one reality, but rather that reality is simply a construct (Guba and Lincoln 1994).

with propositions or hypothesis. These types of studies can, therefore, be expected to end with hypotheses, rather than to test these hypotheses.

The evaluation criteria for this type of research are not well established compared to those from the natural science approach, and it is fairly obvious that the criteria from the natural sciences approach cannot be fully applied. For example, reliability is inappropriate because it is difficult, if not impossible, for another researcher to conduct the same case study again.[12] Criteria in the social sciences paradigm include trustworthiness and authenticity (Denzin and Lincoln 1994, p. 100) and credibility (Janesick 1994, p. 216).[13]

Design Sciences Approach

A third approach has its roots in the design sciences, and is particularly relevant for projects that contribute to practice, see Chapters 4 and 7. This viewpoint differs from the two discussed earlier, in that it isn't primarily concerned with what reality is (a question of: what is?), but rather with designing solutions to practical problems (a question of: does it, that is the solution, work?). This approach is, for example, followed in engineering fields, but also in the field of medicine where a practical solution is sought for a disease. This approach doesn't follow the empirical cycle, but instead a regulative cycle; see Figure 6.2. Especially because businesses are often interested in a solution for its problems, the application of a design (thought-out solution path) may have practical value, leading to a better connection with industry.

One of the mistakes made with projects that make a contribution to practice is that, often a tool or mechanism to, for instance, evaluate

---

[12] Janesick (1994, p. 217) points out "[T]he value of the case study is its uniqueness; consequently, reliability in the traditional sense of replicability is pointless here."

[13] Janesick (1994, p. 214) also mentions "[T]he researcher should describe his or her role thoroughly, so that he reader understands the relationship between the researcher and participants." This goes back to the issue of interpreting the data and, due to the interaction of researcher and participants, the subjectivity. An additional technique to help in this regard is the use of triangulation, that is, use of different methods, researchers, data sources, and so on.

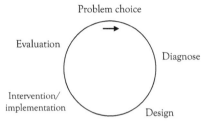

Figure 6.2 The regulative cycle (adapted from Van Strien (1986)

a company's performance is developed to facilitate the solution. Subsequently, this newly developed tool gets applied, and then based on the application, conclusions are drawn about the company's performance. This is a fatal flaw because the study in this instance is not oriented on evaluating whether the tool works correctly, but rather assumes that it does. This assumption is invalid because the tool was not tested or, in other words, the tool was not calibrated. It is like designing a new ruler, putting lines on it in a random fashion and then using this new ruler to determine the length of an object. This is an invalid method because the random lines on the ruler have not been compared with objects of known lengths (calibrating) to determine whether the ruler works appropriately.

In terms of theory, which relates to the quality of the proposed solution and confidence in this particular solution, the regulative cycle approach has severe drawbacks. Jorna (1994) argues that the regulative cycle approach is problematic for business situations because the underlying theories about organizations are not yet well-developed. In other words, because theories about organizational behavior are not developed enough, it is difficult to prescribe a certain design, that is, the solution. For example, companies are not adequately understood to predict whether a business is going to be successful or not. If that knowledge existed, it would have severe implications for financial markets. So, under those circumstances, how can solutions be provided with confidence? Therefore, if the design or solution is implemented, then from a more theoretical perspective, an evaluation of the process shouldn't just be on coming up with the solution. This is an evaluation of the process for undergoing the regulative cycle from Figure 6.2. Instead, to gain

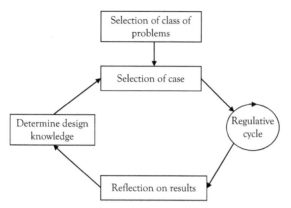

Figure 6.3 The reflective cycle (adapted from van Aken (1994)

theoretical insight, the evaluation should be oriented on: Did the solution work? However, if a solution in one situation is implemented and evaluated, the lessons learned will be limited, as it can be rather specific for that particular situation. To allow some type of generalization from designs and their usefulness, van Aken (1994) developed the reflective cycle; see Figure 6.3.

Van Aken (1994) argues that knowledge in *design science* is created by the interaction between professionals (in practical field) and scientists. The professional solves practical problems, and the scientist analyzes how the professional solves the problem. The professional is aimed at solving one particular problem, and the scientist is aimed at developing scientific knowledge that can be used to solve a class of similar problems. The reflective cycle uses a series of cases to develop design knowledge, based on a reflection of the results. Note that this is not about *what is?*, but rather *does it work?* It is the linking of the results (the success of the implementation) back to the design that is important. This linkage generates knowledge about the particular design that was used, which is useful for the design of solutions in other situations.

The criteria for design sciences are, similar to the social sciences, not well-established. In this regard, due to the often limited number of cases, but in-depth material, it is probably useful to adopt some of the criteria from the approach rooted in the social sciences. However, what has to be kept in mind is that a design-oriented study should look at *does it work?*, rather than at *what is reality?*

A Note on the International Dimension

The three approaches discussed each can be considered valid approaches to research. However, not everybody shares that thought, and there are differences across locations in that regard. For example, the approach rooted in the natural sciences emphasizes quantitative analysis of a few aspects across large samples in order to test hypotheses and make statistical generalizations. Such a view corresponds well with the approach that dominates North American business research (Bengtsson, Elg, and Lind 1997, p. 474). Whereas, business research in Europe more frequently follows the approach rooted in the social sciences (Bengtsson, Elg, and Lind 1997).

Iterative Nature

While there are different approaches to the research aspect of business projects as described, these approaches have common elements. One common element of graduate-level projects is that they are typically iterative in nature. This goes back to the discussion in Chapter 3 and the uncertainties in the environment. It also goes back to the task, discipline, or problem project characteristics discussed in Chapter 4. For the problem-project type, a high degree of self-direction is required. Students may be given some general directions, but the course of action is not planned in detail by the instructor. In these instances, the initial problem formulation provides the initial direction for the research in the project, but as expertise is gained, this gets adjusted and becomes more focused; see Figure 6.4.

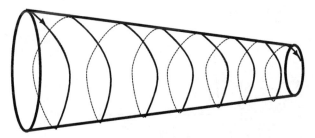

Figure 6.4 The iterative nature of research in projects

Because of the iterative nature of the research, and the uncertainties involved, student teams go through different levels of confidence. At the start of the research in a project, when a few sources are found and read, the confidence is high because with limited sources and understanding, the perception is that it is all understood. As more sources are included, things get complicated because new angles and viewpoints are introduced. Consequently, the confidence in understanding the project drops. Next, through discussion and thinking, students are able to reconcile the differences from the different sources. This means that new insights are gained, and as a consequence, confidence grows. This pattern repeats itself as the project, and the research connected to it develops over time. This is depicted in Figure 6.5. Note that this pattern has several ups and downs, but the overall trend is one of improvement.

This typical pattern of a project can be metaphorically described with a trip through a tunnel. Early on in the project when the topic is selected, typically, a team will feel fairly confident as it is fairly clear what needs to be done, that is, research on a certain topic or designing a solution. This is the road leading up to the tunnel. It still looks sunny outside, and although there is a tunnel ahead, the expectation is that the tunnel is just a small obstacle on the trip. When a team delves into the existing theories and data, things start to become vague as the team has to search for the underlying variables and how things fit together. This is the beginning part of the tunnel. There is, deceptively, still some light from the opening of the tunnel and teams, therefore, have a false sense of security. Over

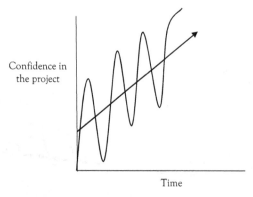

Figure 6.5 Student confidence levels in the research project

time, things may become more confusing. This is the darkest part of the tunnel. But then, things will start to make sense, that is, there is light at the end of the tunnel. By the end of the project, and looking back, the topic is typically understood, and in addition, insight was gained on the trip itself, that is, the tunnel.

Mission Creep

As the project develops over time, another thing to watch out for is mission creep. This is depicted in Figure 6.6. On the one hand, as part of the iterative process, the exact purpose of the project has to become more focused over time. For example, in a consulting-oriented project (a project that contributes to practice), it may be necessary to refine what will exactly be part of the project, while in a theory-oriented project, it may be a matter of refining it to end up with a feasible project that can be conducted during an academic term. This means that the initial purpose of the project stays the same in a way, but the focus becomes narrower. For example, focusing on a limited number of the relevant variables or using a smaller and more specific sample. Mission creep occurs when the target is changed by, for example, moving in different directions. This is often a side-effect in projects. In consulting-oriented projects, this can occur as new data and insights can lead to new directions. Similarly, in theory-oriented projects, when new insights are gained, new ideas develop, which may be deemed more interesting or feasible. This process, however, does not typically end because once a new direction is established, this process tends to repeat itself. It is, therefore, advisable to make a decision for the general *target* for the project and stick to this target. This is especially

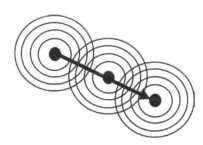

Figure 6.6 Mission creep

important for classroom projects where there is limited time. It should also be kept in mind that the main purpose of the project is often not the end result of the project but rather the process involved. Furthermore, related to this the application and development of critical skills is more important from an educational perspective.

Conclusion

Classroom projects have a research component. This applies to projects that contribute to theory, for which it is often explicit. It also applies to projects that contribute to practice. It involves research on theories as well as on data. It is important to realize that research is *not* simply finding and regurgitating information from other sources. Especially at the graduate, level critical thinking is expected, and this means creating something new. Information was provided on three general approaches for research. Generally, projects that are contributing to practice will follow an approach that is similar to the regulative cycle. Projects that are contributing to theory will follow an approach that follows the empirical cycle, but depending on the purpose of the project, it may cover different parts of this cycle. For sake of completeness, another cycle, that is the reflective cycle, was also discussed. This cycle is unlikely to be followed in classroom projects because it requires classes of problems, in other words, many projects.

Students should be aware of the iterative nature of classroom projects, and with it, how confidence in the project, and also the project team performance, experiences ups and downs over time. Another issue raised was that of the danger and potential of mission creep. It takes conscious effort to make sure that the project team stays on target.

CHAPTER 7

Projects that Contribute to Practice

As was explained in Chapter 4, there are different types of projects. This chapter deals with projects that contribute to practice. This means that they have a real, or imagined, client and often deals with researching solutions to problems or alternatives, or opportunities. The chapter is an extension of the previous two chapters that covered teams and the general research aspect. In Chapter 3, the five basic process of projects were covered, and it was shown that these processes apply in different types of environments, although the sequencing of these processes may differ; see also Figure 3.5. A characteristic for projects that contribute to practice is that it deals with the customer. Therefore, the setup of this chapter is oriented on the basic processes, that is, initiating, planning, executing, monitoring and control, and closing (PMI 2017a).[1] For these processes, the deliverables during these processes to the customer are covered, and the structural elements for those deliverables to the client are provided. These deliverables can be viewed as a type of scaffolding. Scaffolding is used in education, but the concept comes from the construction industry. In the construction industry, scaffolding is a temporary structure built to help with construction of buildings. Scaffolding is often seen as

---

[1] Trilling and Ginevri (2017) provide a convenient comparison of the project lifecycle terms typically used in life, learning, and career skills. See Table 7.1 for a review of the common terms. The key to moving forward is that the terms may change from one skill set to the next, but the concepts underlying the terms are common across life, learning, and career skills. This is an important point: what is being learned in project-based learning is directly applicable to someone's career, but it requires being open to understanding the common threads running through projects in life, learning, and career in order to keep life-long learning alive.

Table 7.1 Common terms across skill sets (adapted from Trilling and Ginevri 2017)

Life skills	Learning skills		Career skills
Project steps (Four steps)	Project cycle (Four phases)		Project methodology (Five processes) (PMI, 2017)
• Set a goal • Plan the steps • Do it • Review it	• Define • Plan • Do • Review		• Initiating • Planning • Executing • Monitoring and Controlling • Closing
	Prescriptive • Identify • Design • Create • Evaluate	Exploratory • Imagine • Discover • Model • Evolve	Agile-Adaptive • Envision • Speculate • Explore • Adapt • Close

interconnected pipes supporting boards or platforms around the outside of a building under construction. Scaffolding gives workers an access to parts of the building that ordinarily are unreachable. Once the construction is finished, scaffolding is removed, and the building is self-sustaining. Scaffolding is a common educational technique to help students bridge gaps in understanding and knowledge (Great Schools Partnership 2015; Savery 2015). Scaffolding could come in the form of templates, rubrics, or examples of similar work (van Rooij 2009). So, in this chapter, several such templates and examples are provided.

Initiate

The deliverable for the initiate process is the charter. The charter is the first formal recognition of the project by the project team. The charter is a short and simple document that explains why the project is being undertaken, what the project will produce, how long it will take, who is represented in the team, and to what client (the instructor or project sponsor) the team is responsible. For the student project team, there is some overlap between the team contracts (discussed in Chapter 5) and the charter. The important difference is that the charter is necessary while working with a client, whereas a team contract is more directed toward the internal workings of the team.

Purpose

The charter is "a document issued by the project initiator or sponsor that formally authorizes the existence of a project and provides the project manager with the authority to apply organizational resources to project activities" (PMI 2017a, p. 715). In a school setting, the charter is done by the project team with input from the instructor and the client. The instructor will usually provide a template or rubric by which the team can be guided in completing a charter.

Approach

Although the charter is to be done relatively quickly and be a rough approximation of the plan, there is one part of the charter that requires particular focus. This one part is the business case, that is the feasibility and benefits of the project. The business case may not be specifically called the business case in all charters, but the key components of a business case should be included in all charters. These components go by different names that are aligned with different methods, but the concepts are the same (Herman and Siegelaub 2009; IIBA 2015; PMI 2017a). In the project management body of knowledge (PMBOK), there are two documents that precede the charter, the needs assessment and the benefits management plan (PMI 2017a). The business analysis body of knowledge (BABOK), recognizes three types of requirements; business, stakeholder, and solution requirements. The PRINCE2 (2009) identifies outputs, outcomes, and benefits. The significance of these various components is captured in the Logical Framework Approach's (NORAD 1999) assignment of goal, purpose, and outputs to the cause-and-effect relationship of the strategic, organizational, and project objectives.

Essentially, the project produces some product or service or solution that is tangible or present and is called an output. The output allows the realization of some outcome or benefit. The outcome or benefit is the near-term impact from the use of or implementation of the project output. The benefits derived then begin to satisfy the business at a strategic level by helping to achieve the strategic objectives. For example, a training project leads to more competent employees (the benefit), which contributes to a well-run business (strategic objective) measured in profitability. One can see the terminology can be rather convoluted and confusing, and part of what must be done during the project is embracing the terminology used in the firm and bringing it into the business case. The key concepts that must be captured in the business case, irrespective of the language used, are what is the project producing, what benefit is derived from the project being successful, and how does this all fit with the strategic plan of the business? This all requires the project team to understand a broad range of business objectives that not only define the project, but also the business. Some projects can get caught up in the lure of technology and fail to find alignment with organizational objectives. Some projects have too broad of an approach and fail to find the specific products needed to support the big ideas. The business logic conveyed in the business case is probably the most important component of the entire project. This is why, the charter is a very important part of a successful project.

The second most important part of a charter is a stakeholder analysis. The stakeholder analysis "determines whose interests should be taken into account throughout the project" (PMI 2017a, p. 723). After thorough data collection and analysis, stakeholder information is often presented as a grid showing stakeholders' power versus interest, power versus influence, or impact versus influence. This can lead to a prioritization of stakeholders and the basis for a communications plan with stakeholders (PMI 2017a). News headlines are rampant with examples of stakeholders who were missed in drawing up plans, but become very obvious when they voice their concerns after the project has started or been completed.

The charter should also include a description of the product and the work necessary to produce it. The project team should be introduced, and roles explained if they have been determined. Milestones, or important transitions from one phase to the next, need to be estimated using dates. The charter is the first opportunity to document basic assumptions (the known unknowns) and the associated high-level risks. Although most school projects do not incur costs, if certain resources are estimated to be necessary for the project, they should also be listed. And finally, a brief summary of team policies and communication methods needs to be agreed upon and documented in the charter. The charter is usually signed-off by the team members, project manager, and sponsor.

Implications and Practical Tips

Festina lente is an old Latin phrase that translates as *make haste, slowly.* The charter is the slowness injected into the start of a project that pays off later. The charter is a necessary step that gets a project going in the right direction. It is a little daunting that such an important part of the project is usually entrusted to a new team with little experience of working together. Team development and meeting facilitation skills should be exercised with careful discipline. Additionally, a team needs to be instantly communicating clearly and efficiently. A file storage and file versioning system must be accessible to all team members. There are a variety of popular project messaging applications available that allow file sharing and message archiving. Such applications separate out messages from e-mails where things can get lost or misplaced. Ground rules should be set up around expectations of message response times, language conventions, and general netiquette.

Another skill practiced during the charter is interviewing. A project sponsor or instructor will expect a team to ask a lot of questions in order to grasp the essence of organizational strategies, the purpose guiding the project, and the depth and breadth of resources needed to undertake the project. Interviews should be structured around key questions. It is recommended that two people should interview a *client* or stakeholder. One person can ask questions while the other is taking notes, recording the conversation, or providing counterpoint to the main line of questioning. Interview notes should always be transcribed immediately after the interview. Valuable insights get lost over time.

A literature review on relevant theories and related aspects is essential. Although the literature review may not be featured in the product one produces for a project, that is the report, the knowledge and terminology gained through a literature review can make a tremendous difference in attaining the needed focus on a subject. Articles, books, blogs, and videos should all be collected and organized for access by all team members.

In addition to the charter, several other documents may come into play in the initiate stage of a project, which relate to legal aspects. Projects that take place within courses, but that involve real clients expose, the parties involved to legal concerns. In some universities, the legal team from the university is involved, while at other universities, this may be handled by the instructor. If a legal team is involved, it is likely that there will be a general type of contract that spells out several issues that may, for example, include the use of the university name, things about the length of time of the project, the educational purpose of the project, and so on. More commonly, when the project team has to visit a company, there may be the potential for liability, for example, a student tripping and getting injured on the company premises, or alternatively, the student tripping and damaging the company's equipment. An example of a waiver for such an event is provided in Appendix B. Another legal document is a nondisclosure form. Clients frequently have concerns about the confidentiality of the information that they share with outsiders such as a student project team. Therefore, they may ask the team as well as the instructor and sometimes even administrators of the university to sign a nondisclosure agreement. A couple of examples of nondisclosure forms are provided in Appendix C.

Example

A charter sample outline is provided in Table 7.2, and a short example of a student charter is provided in Appendix D. Note that the sample provided in Appendix D is an abbreviated version of the sample outline. The project team should tailor the charter to their situation. But, answering the basic questions of why, what, who, and when, is a minimum.

It was explained in Chapter 6 that (classroom) projects have iterative characteristics. For instance, progressive elaboration is "the iterative process of increasing the level of detail in a project management plan as greater amounts of information and more accurate estimates become available" (PMI 2017a, p. 715). Table 7.3 shows how the project was progressively elaborated during the initiation phase of the project. The column on the left is an early draft, and the column on the right is what the team agreed upon for the plan.

What stands out in the preceding comparison is the agreement on the higher-level objectives. The team clearly understands the overall strategy and who they want impacted. What they do not clearly understand are

Table 7.2 General outline for a charter

Topic	Subtopic
Background	Client strategy
	Business case
Product or project description	High-level objectives
	Outputs and activities
Team	
Schedule (milestone dates)	
Assumptions and risks	
Resources needed	
Team policies	
Communication plan	
Sign-offs	

Table 7.3 Progressive elaboration of project objectives

First draft	Final draft
Goal Protect children	**Goal** Protect children
Purpose Educate parents	**Purpose** Educate parents
Outputs 1. Published curriculum 2. Trained parents 3. Project management	**Outputs** 1. Published curriculum 2. Trained parents 3. Project management
Activities 1.1 Determine topics to cover 1.2 Research topics 1.3 Develop 1.4 Test 1.5 Revise 1.6 Review 1.7 Finalize 1.8 Present 2.1 Determine location for training 2.2 Determine equipment required for delivery 2.3 Advertise training 2.4 Pretest 2.5 Present training 2.6 Post-test	**Activities** 1.1 Modules 1.2 Technologies 1.3 Legalities 1.4 Curriculum 1.5 Test 1.6 Validate 1.7 Publish 2.1 Danger training 2.2 Protection training 2.3 Parental training

(Continued)

Table 7.3 (Continued)

First draft	Final draft
3.1 Project charter	3.1 Form team
3.2 Project plan	3.2 Select project
3.3 2 x Status reports	3.3 Project charter
3.4 Evaluation report	3.4 Project plan
	3.5 Status report 1
	3.6 Status report 2
	3.7 Evaluation report
	3.8 Record results

the exact steps needed to get there. Sometimes, a team will have the exact opposite situation. They will clearly understand what and how they want to do the project, but do not know ultimately why they are doing it. A team with a strong technological background may feel compelled to exercise their technological muscles at the expense of providing value. In a project planning situation, gaining consensus at the higher-level objectives first makes finding the right solutions at the output and activities level much more aligned with the group's strategic outlook (Norad 2008).

Progressive elaboration is evident at the activities level. Notice the activity items on the right are more deliverable-oriented than the actions on the left. The team's understanding has matured on the right, and this is demonstrated by defining the deliverables the team will provide. It appears some of the topics that were undetermined at the time of the writing on the left are being specified on the right. Another level of activities is now assumed, but not specified, below those activities listed on the right. The 2.x level activities on the left could be represented by an activity on the right called *training preparation*. However, it seems the team has assumed those activities as a part of the three types of training listed on the right. "The WBS is a detailed hierarchical listing of all of the things that must be delivered and all of the activities that must be carried out to complete the project" (PMIEF 2016, p. 66). The WBS on the right has much more depth of planning than the one on the left. But, much of it is undocumented. This is both good and bad. It is good because one should only plan enough to accomplish the objectives. However, it is bad in the sense that there is a lot unspecified. This could hurt the team if key people had to leave the project, or there are team members without the knowledge or skills assumed by the plan. Either way, the plan on the right shows progression and could be further refined. In the hundreds of student evaluations of projects that we have read, the most common comment is that students wished they had spent more time on the initiate stage of the project and on understanding and refining the WBS. Their typical comment is that it would have made the whole project easier.

Plan

Planning is the second basic process in projects, and the deliverable is a plan that is a detailed extension of the charter. It specifies, at a minimum, exactly what is going to be done, by whom, and how long it is going to take.

Purpose

The plan is "the document that describes how the project will be executed, monitored and controlled, and closed" (PMI 2017a, p. 716).

Approach

The natural tendency is to want to start working on the project as soon as possible, and typically, this leads to scheduling things prematurely and going after symptoms of the problem, rather than the underlying issues (Harvard Business Review 2016). Therefore, respect the words of wisdom and take the time to get things right (make a plan), and the team will increase their chances of realizing success in meeting their objectives (Davis and Atkinson 2010). If the team has a charter, then they are well on their way to developing a plan. The plan is an opportunity to reuse and expand upon the work that went into the charter.

The most important component of the plan is the work breakdown structure (WBS). The hierarchical listing is a subdividing of deliverables into smaller more manageable parts. For example, a study for a client may include a report document and an oral presentation. The report document is decomposed into its parts such as an introduction, a business case, a market analysis, a financial analysis, and an implementation plan for the proposed product development. Each of these parts can be further broken down to smaller sections or phases of development. The oral presentation is also broken down into slides and a script. The slides may need to be further broken down into the respective topics of the report document. As also aforementioned in the definition, project activities such as the plan, the progress reports, team meetings, and the lessons learned debrief are also part of the WBS. Although decomposing functional deliverables in a top-down approach is probably the most typical way of developing a WBS, using phases to break up the project in a sequential fashion is another. Other projects may lend themselves to a geographical breakdown or a sub-systems breakdown depending of the centralized or distributed nature of the project (PMI 2006). See Figure 7.1 for an example WBS of a proposed product development project.

The WBS should be broken down to a level of detail that allows team members to make informed estimates of the WBS elements' durations. For example, in the report document, there is item 1.2, the business case. This certainly can be broken into more manageable (in terms of how long it will take) pieces, and each of those pieces may need even more decomposition. As mentioned, the business case is made up of at least three components; the business requirements or strategic objectives involved, the stakeholder requirements or the near-term impact expected to result from the project, and the solutions requirements or specifications of the project's final product or service. In addition to the acquiring the information required for those three sections, there will be meetings

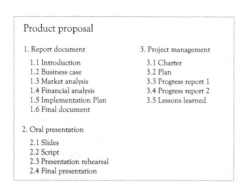

Figure 7.1 High-level WBS for a product proposal

```
1.2 Business case
    1.2.1 Business documents review meeting
    1.2.2 Business requirements draft
    1.2.3 Stakeholders requirements draft
    1.2.4 Solutions requirements draft
    1.2.5 Review of draft
    1.2.6 Draft revisions
    1.2.7 Final draft submission to report
```

Figure 7.2 WBS decomposition of the business case

and review sessions involved to coordinate with the other parts of the document and finalize the business case. See Figure 7.2 for an example of how the business case can be decomposed into smaller deliverables or actual work packages.

One can see in Figure 7.2, that all of the things that must be delivered and all of the activities that must be carried out to complete the business case have been listed (PMIEF 2016, p. 66). A team member should feel comfortable that all team members are aware of what it takes to accomplish each of items 1.2.1 through 1.2.7. A word of warning: too much detail can overwhelm team members. Typically, breakdowns should be limited to no more than seven elements per level, and the levels should be minimized. Each additional WBS level injects more complexity. If the team is new to projects or does not know each other's capabilities, then more detail may be necessary to help communicate the project to each other and stakeholders. But, ultimately, keep it as simple as possible. One thing that helps is producing a WBS dictionary. The WBS dictionary is "a document that provides detailed deliverable, activity, and scheduling information about each component in the work breakdown structure" (PMI 2017a, p. 726). As one becomes more experienced in defining a WBS, then one can feel more confident that just the right amount of planning and decomposition is being done, not too much and not too little. In agile environments, this kind of experience is expected of team members as they necessarily become more self-directed. The WBS is important because it becomes the basis for most of the key planning techniques we use in the plan. The following sections will show how the WBS is used to help assign responsibilities, develop a schedule, and account for resources.

People make the project, so assigning people to the WBS work starts to bring more reality to the project. A popular technique that combines the

WBS with the people involved in the project is the responsibility assignment matrix (RAM). The people section of the plan should include the roles and responsibility of each team member and a RAM. See Figure 7.3 for an example of the RAM for the business case. Kim and Jan are working to develop the drafts. Syd is editing the drafts together and preparing the final document. As people are assigned to various works and responsibilities, they may discover alternatives to how the work was originally envisioned. Plans are "progressively elaborated" (PMI 2017a, p. 715), in the sense that as new or better ways of doing the project are discovered, the changes are incorporated into the plan. The planning process is iterative.

The schedule also utilizes the WBS in two ways to better communicate the project, with a network diagram and a Gantt chart. The WBS is not necessarily listed in a sequential form. Thus, the temporal logic (what order in which work is done) is communicated in a network diagram. One simply takes all the lowest-level components of the WBS and puts them in a sequential order that makes sense. If people are available, doing work concurrently is a good way of shortening the time needed to get things done. Again, determining the best network diagram is an iterative process. See Figure 7.4 for an example of a network diagram for the business case.

The most common way of communicating a project schedule is with a Gantt chart. The WBS components are listed against a time scale. Each component is represented by a bar on the time scale. The length of the bar shows the duration of the component. Interactions of the components are

	Kim	Jan	Syd
1.2 Business case			
1.2.1 Business documents review meeting	A	R	C
1.2.2 Business requirements draft	A	R	C
1.2.3 Stakeholders requirements draft	R	A	C
1.2.4 Solutions requirements draft	R	A	C
1.2.5 Review of drafts	C	C	R/A
1.2.6 Draft revisions	C	C	R/A
1.2.7 Final draft submission to report	C	C	R/A
	R = Responsible, A = Accountable, C = Consult, I = Inform		

Figure 7.3 RAM for the business case

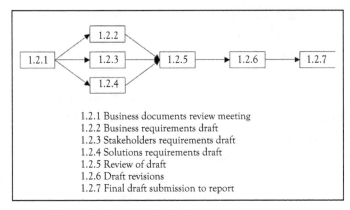

1.2.1 Business documents review meeting
1.2.2 Business requirements draft
1.2.3 Stakeholders requirements draft
1.2.4 Solutions requirements draft
1.2.5 Review of draft
1.2.6 Draft revisions
1.2.7 Final draft submission to report

Figure 7.4 Network diagram for the business case

	Week 1	Week 2	Week 3	Week 4	Week 5
1.2 Business case					
1.2.1 Business documents review meeting	X				
1.2.2 Business requirements draft		XXXXX			
1.2.3 Stakeholders requirements draft		XXXXX			
1.2.4 Solutions requirements draft		XXXXX			
1.2.5 Review of drafts			XXXXX		
1.2.6 Draft revisions				XXXXX	
1.2.7 Final draft submission to report					X
	X = One day				

Figure 7.5 Gantt chart for the business case

not as easily seen on the Gantt chart, but the Gantt chart is an excellent diagram for showing what is planned versus what actually happens as the project progresses. See an example of the Gantt chart for the business case in Figure 7.5. Project management software typically provides easy ways of showing schedules. However, post-it notes can be used to develop network diagrams, and a spreadsheet may suffice for developing a Gantt chart.

In the event that the project will need some kind of materials and supplies beyond paper, pens, and laptops, then account for this with the WBS. List the resources with the associated WBS component and separately as a resource list. Provide a monetary cost, if necessary. Most schools do not provide funding for projects. In such cases, where the team does put up funding for the project, tracking the costs for the sake of the team is a good idea.

The communications plan and stakeholder analysis done in the charter should be updated and included in the plan. The parts of the plan described so far are a minimum for a project plan. Add subsidiary sections (like a risk plan) to the plan as needed. Plans should be complete, concise, and consistent. All parts of the plan should be easy to edit and change as the project progressively elaborates. Use a web-based software office suite that can accommodate the entire team. Keep both project and product work transparent, meaning everyone should be able to see each other's progress. As the plan morphs, save consecutive versions of the plan with a numbering system so that the team members have a record of earlier ideas, and the origin of changes can be traced.

Present the plan for approval and get the necessary sign-offs. The team should have kept key stakeholders informed during the plan preparation so that approval is mostly a formality. Otherwise, the team should be prepared for revisions and resubmitting the plan for approval in order to execute the project.

Implications

A major problem in many plans is a failure to account for changes, from two perspectives. First, the physical layout of the planning documents, tables, figures, and charts should be such that they can be easily edited. As old-fashioned as it may sound, whiteboards and post-its provide a simple easy-to-edit system for planning and tracking a project. If the plan is not easy to edit, then it will not be edited, and the purpose for planning is lost. On large projects, one person can be dedicated to running the project management software. Or, in distributed projects, those responsible submit their portion of the project to a central repository for coordination. At least one person on a project should be designated as the editor of planning documents and charts. Second, the other perspective on accounting for change deals with the change process. The plan should stipulate who can request a change, review a change, and approve a change. Changes to plans usually mean more work. More work comes at a cost to the project and must be carefully considered as being appropriate by the key stakeholders. One thing that can anticipate change is to place buffers, or slack time after or between the scheduling of major deliverables. Building in

Table 7.4 General plan outline

Topic	Subtopic
Introduction	
Business case	
Project scope	WBS
	WBS dictionary
Team members	Roles and responsibilities
	RAM
Schedule	Network diagram
	Gantt chart
Resources	
Communications	
Stake holders	
Risks (optional)	
Quality (optional)	

slack allows a part of the project to run a little long without threatening the overall project schedule. And lastly, as much as planning and project management can help a project, too much planning and project management can get in the way. All this planning is to support the project, not be the project. The best amount of planning is just enough planning.

Example

A sample student plan is provided in Appendix E. Note that, in this example, the students assigned hourly rates to determine an estimated budget. The budget was used for tracking purposes and does not reflect a real project cost. Microsoft Project was used to generate Gantt charts, network diagrams, and budgets. A general outline for a plan document is provided in Table 7.4.

Execute

The deliverable for the execute process is the same as that for the monitor and control process, that is, a progress report. The progress report will be covered in the next section. Instead of this particular deliverable, the focus will be on some of the work that students will have to carry out during the execute phase. Typically, in order to help the client, the project team will have to apply theories and models that are part of the course materials, for example, when analyzing a situation. Understanding the theory and applying it correctly is of critical importance.

Purpose

In order to solve problems, come up with solutions, or to develop new insights for the client, it is necessary to apply the theories and models that are part of the educational background of the student team. This is, after all, one of the main reasons for companies to get help, that is, to have the student team apply the latest methods and techniques. This is also where synergy occurs and where value gets added through project-based learning because the students get to apply the theories.

Approach

In order to correctly apply theories, models, methods, or techniques, the student team will first have to make sure that they have sufficient understanding of these business tools. Once they possess an adequate level of understanding, then it has to be correctly applied. In some instances, this process can be somewhat hidden for a client, for example when the project deliverable is an Internet-based administrative system, that is, a program. In other instances, this process will be more visible to the client, for example when the project deliverable is a written (strategic) plan. In either situation, the importance is that the theories are followed or if deviation occurs, that this is explained.

The application of models requires a fair amount of data collection. There are different types of data, both primary and secondary. Primary data is data the team directly collects. Secondary data is the data that already exists, or in other words, it comes from other sources. Secondary data is in many cases sufficient for the necessary analysis and synthesis to create viable report information. The discussion of literature reviews should help in this respect. If primary data is used, then it needs to be carefully planned. Primary data collection of information on human subjects may also require approval by a university Institutional Review Board. Whether the team is collecting data via experimentation, survey, or interviews, there are rigorous designs and standards by which the team should be guided. It is best to source a guide for the type of data collection the team chooses and confirm methods with the instructor before implementing the collection process. Faulty methods can undermine the best intentions, so it is important to take the time to know the pros and cons of any method the team undertakes.

Implications

Educational programs, such as an MBA program, provide students with many theories, models, methods, and techniques. These can all be considered business tools that help companies with decision making. In a project, they are typically used to help with the development of a plan, application or design of a solution. It involves five steps: select, explain, apply, assume, and conclude.

For any given task that requires the application of a tool in some sort of analysis, the first task is to select an appropriate tool. Students learn many tools, and it is, therefore, imperative to know and understand the conditions under which the tool can be applied. Needless to say that the correct application of an incorrect tool is meaningless. For example, when dealing with inventory control techniques, a popular method to apply is the economic-order quantity model. However, this model assumes that demand is constant over time. In situations where the demand is not constant over time, it is, therefore, not appropriate to apply this model. The project team has to *justify* the selection of the tool they choose to use and provide the source for this tool. Understanding the assumptions under which the model can be used is a major component of critical thinking and meaningful analysis (Brookfield 2012).

Depending on the sort of project deliverable and knowledge of the client, the selected tool may have to be explained to the client, for instance, in the final project report. If this explanation takes up a lot of space, then it is recommended to move the explanation to the appendix so that it doesn't distract from the findings, which is what the clients are typically interested in.

With the tool in place, the next step is a correct application of the tool. This is an absolutely critical exercise and the quality of a project often stands or falls with this application. It goes back to an adequate understanding of the tool. Sometimes, students end up with analysis that is too superficial because they either do not have a full grasp of the tool or because they apply it too superficially. In this latter instance, it becomes more of a guessing or brainstorming exercise, rather than a meaningful and critical analysis. For instance, in terms of strategic analysis, many students have learned about the five-forces model by Porter (1980). It should be understood that this model is a tool to determine the overall attractiveness of an industry, that is, its overall profitability potential and what is causing it. It is one of the two steps for strategic analysis for Porter; the other step is positioning the company in such a way that above-average returns can be expected (Magretta 2012). A superficial application of this tool is one where a team notes the five forces and then comes up with items that they think may apply to the situation. This type of guessing is a demonstration of not fully grasping the meaning of business tools and can be dangerous to the client company. A correct application of this tool requires an in-depth understanding of the tool. Porter (1980) provides specific advice on the *sub-variables* that are part of the tool for each of the five forces, and which, therefore, should be analyzed. For instance, for the *threat of entry* force, Porter (1980) recognizes *barriers to entry* as just one of the factors that determine threat to entry. Other factors include: expected retaliation, entry deterring price, and for instance, experience and scale as entry barriers. Furthermore, the *barriers to entry* is divided into another seven major sources: economies of scale, product differentiation, capital requirements, switching costs, access to distribution channels, cost disadvantages independent of scale, and government policy. The correct application of the five-forces model, therefore, requires an assessment of all of these sources of barriers to entry. This allows an assessment of the barriers of entry. This, combined with the other factors such as the expected retaliation, allows an assessment of the threat of entry force. When this assessment is combined with a similar detailed application and assessment of the other forces, the overall industry can be assessed and understood.

When business tools such as the five-forces model are appropriately understood and correctly applied, this means that data is required. The business tool should drive the data collection. In many situations, the full application of the model requires data that is not available. Sometimes, due to the missing data, students ignore the associated variables and do not discuss this in, for example, the final report. This is a fatal flaw. It is crucial to inform the client of any missing data that may have influenced the outcome of the project! Therefore, it is strongly recommended to make explicit assumptions, for example, numbering them in the text, about the variables for which no data exist so that the client can assess the risk related to not having sufficient data. For instance, in the previous discussion, the *threat of entry*, if no data is available for the factor *expected retaliation,* then an assumption can be made such as: "assumption 1 is that due to the high number of firms and the fragmented nature of the industry, the expected retaliation of competitors is low."

Last, after the correct application of the business tool, conclusions should be drawn. This is part of the value that is created for the client company.

Example

An abbreviated example of the application of a business tool is provided in Appendix F. In this instance, a project team was working with a made-up client, that is, a real company (Jimmy John's), but not an actual client of the project. The example concerns the application of a business tool to analyze the macro environment, that is, the PEST model. Only the first portion of the application of this PEST model is provided, that is, an analysis of the political situation.

What this example shows is that the project team identifies the need to analyze the macro environment; they do this in Section 2.1. They also present the tool for this analysis in an accompanying figure and provide the source for this tool. The following Figure F.1 is their justification for the use of this particular tool. For the analysis of the political environment, (Section 2.2), they first provide a short explanation of this part of the tool (Section 2.2.1) and then have an in-depth application of the model. Note that, in the figure, eight aspects of the political environment are identified and the team discusses exactly those eight aspects in Sections 2.2.2 through 2.2.9. In their analysis of these eight aspects, they generally provide the sources for their information and data. They combine their insight from the eight aspects in Section 2.2.10 to draw conclusions about the political environment. Although not provided in the example, they analyze the other three parts of the PEST tool in a similar fashion and then draw their overall conclusions about the macro environment in Section 2.6.

Monitor and Control

During the monitor and control process, similar to the execute process, the deliverables to the clients are progress reports. Progress reports are released by the project team during the project to communicate how closely the project is meeting the estimates laid out in the plan.

Purpose

Progress reports are "work performance information ... which is intended to generate decisions or raise issues, actions, or awareness" (PMI 2017a, p. 26).

Approach

Managing stakeholders' information expectations can be done through progress reports. And, as stakeholders, this includes internal stakeholders such as team members, instructor, and client, and external stakeholders who will be impacted by the project or using the product. Progress reports use the plan as much as possible as a point of departure. The progress report structure can mimic the plan, but in a more compact style. Progress reports must convey the most up-to-date information, and therefore must be done quickly and concisely. A standard format should be established and used consistently for the benefit of both the person putting it together and the reader. The key purpose of the progress report is to help compare the plan to what is actually happening. The plan was the agreed upon path for the project. If there is a deviation from that path, everyone should be aware and help find ways to manage the project scope, team status, schedule, resource needs, and risks that have arisen. The team did its best to anticipate the project, but there will always be changes. Managing the change is communicated in the progress report.

The progress report uses the plan as a project check list. The team can go through the plan and ask the questions:

- Does this component of the plan still hold true?
- If not, why not and what was, or needs, to be done?
- So, in terms of the business case, is the reason for doing the project still viable?
- Is the product and its components still as specified?
- Have any components of the WBS been added, changed, or deleted?
- Are the team members performing as expected and fulfilling responsibilities?
- Are work packages being done in the order and in the timeframe that were estimated?
- Are resources available and as specified?
- Have any anticipated or unknown risks become real?
- Do the risks pose to impact the scope, people, schedule, or resources involved in the project, and if so, how much?

Conveying information in the progress report is summarized well with the tracking Gantt chart. The tracking Gantt chart is just like the Gantt chart in the plan with the addition of markings showing when the work actually happened. In keeping with the business case example, see Figure 7.6, after three weeks of work. Unfortunately, the business

	Week 1	Week 2	Week 3	Week 4	Week 5
1.2 Business case					
1.2.1 Business documents review meeting	X				
1.2.2 Business requirements draft		XXXXX 00	000		
1.2.3 Stakeholders requirements draft		XXXXX 00	000		
1.2.4 Solutions requirements draft		XXXXX 00	000		
1.2.5 Review of drafts			XXXXX 00000		
1.2.6 Draft revisions				XXXXX	
1.2.7 Final draft submission to report					X
	X = One day (planned) 0 = One day (actual)				

Figure 7.6 Tracking Gantt chart in the end of week three progress report

documents review meeting was postponed for a week. This pushed back the three drafts into week three. Syd started the review of the drafts even though they are not complete, in the hope of staying on schedule. The team won't know how well that worked out until they start week four. Syd may have to extend the review of draft revisions. The team built in two days of slack time, Monday and Tuesday, in week five (note the X, "Final draft submission to report," in week five is scheduled on Wednesday, third day of the work week), before the final draft submission, just in case there was a delay. They may have to use that extra time. Building in the extra time was a good way to mitigate a potential delay in the schedule.

Implications

Unfortunately, bad news has a bad reputation. In managing projects, bad news has to be welcomed and anticipated, not because it is wanted, but because bad news is valuable information. Progress reports often bear bad news of missed schedules, unavailable resources (people get sick), or unanticipated issues (lost or corrupted data). Hiding bad news is the worst thing someone can do during project execution. Information is needed to keep the team, project sponsor, and key stakeholders up to date. Creativity and leadership can help save a project, if project information is transparent and available. An often-overlooked aspect of managing a project is recognition and rewards. Large and small accomplishments during the project should be rewarded appropriately. The reward should be something that is of value to team members and the team as a whole (PMI 2017a). Pizza seems to be a universal reward.

Example

An outline for a progress report is shown in Table 7.5, while a sample student progress report is provided in Appendix G.

Close

The deliverable for the closing process is the lessons learned. The lessons learned is a report that brings together all the things the team did well and

Table 7.5 General outline for a progress report

Topic	Subtopic
Introduction	
Update	Business case
	Changes to WBS, team, and resources
Schedule	Update
	Tracking Gantt chart

what can be improved. The lessons learned is the basis for learning and continuous improvement of individuals, team, and organization.

Purpose

Lessons learned is "the knowledge gained during a project which shows how project events were addressed or should be addressed in the future for the purpose of improving future performance" (PMI 2017a, p. 709).

Approach

From an educational context, there are three parts of effective evaluation for learning projects, product results, progress in learning, and process quality (Trilling and Ginevri 2017). To support continuous improvement, each individual team member, team, and organization supporting the team should all contribute to the three-part evaluation. An easy way to do this is by creating a lessons learned register at the start of the project and adding to it as lessons are learned (PMI 2017a). The various products and process can be looked at from two perspectives, what worked and what can be improved (Snyder 2013). The instructor should collect all lessons learned registers and compile them in a lessons learned repository for future teams to review before embarking on a project (PMI 2017a).

Implications

A disciplined approach to progress reports can really pay off for a team when it comes time to produce a final evaluation report or lessons learned.

The progress reports and the memory that gets revived and brought to life is lessons learned. Things like, "We started capturing the audio of our status reports in addition to the charts and tables we posted online" can turn into a major change in practice and increase communication effectiveness. Passing along insights to future teams through lessons learned captures the knowledge gained. However, like a lot of things, it is not quite that simple. When dealing with knowledge management and people, one must take into account motivations, culture, and environment.

> ... knowledge management is about making sure the skills, experience, and expertise of the project team and other stakeholder are used before, during, and after the project Because knowledge resides in the minds of people and people cannot be forced to share what they know (or to pay attention to others' knowledge), the most important part of knowledge management is creating an atmosphere of trust so that people are motivated to share their knowledge. Even the best knowledge management tools and techniques will not work if people are not motivated to share what they know or to pay attention to what others know (PMI 2017a, p. 100).

Example

A simple lessons learned form is provided in Table 7.6. A sample student lessons learned report is provided in Appendix H. Note that this report includes an evaluation of the schedule and budget in addition to evaluating the project impact and lessons learned.

The Agile or Adaptive Approach

As mentioned in Chapter 3, the complexity and uncertainty surrounding many knowledge-worker projects has given rise to an agile or adaptive approach to projects. For a student who is introduced to new content and processes for the first time in a school project, the same type of complexity and uncertainty is manifested. For this reason, it is important for the student to be aware of the agile or adaptive options available that

Table 7.6 Lessons learned form (adapted from Snyder 2013)

Lessons Learned

Project title: _____   Date prepared: _____

	What worked well	What can be improved
Requirements definition and management		
Scope definition and management		
Schedule development and control		
Team development and performance		
Communication management		
Stakeholder management		
Reporting		
Process improvement information		
Product-specific information		
Other		

can turn a prescriptive lifecycle approach into something of a hybrid approach. With this awareness, complexity and uncertainty can be approached with more confidence than what otherwise may feel like staring into a dark unknown. The adaptive approach should not be thought of being any less disciplined than the predictive approach. It may seem more casual in being less predictive, but the flexibility is still supported by practices that need to be respected and sustained throughout the project. The next sections introduce some of the practices associated with an adaptive approach.

Purpose

The agile lifecycle is "an approach that is both iterative and incremental to refine work items and deliver frequently" (PMI 2017b, p. 150).

Approach

The project charter is, again, the important start to the project. And, again there are the business-case questions that must be answered in the charter: (1) Why are we doing this project? (This is the project vision.) (2) Who benefits and how? (This is part of the project purpose.) (3) What does "done" mean for the project? (These are the project's release or grading criteria.) (4) How are we going to work together? (This explains the intended flow of work.) (PMI 2017b, p. 49). In cases where the team may be composed of people who have never worked together on a project, a team charter may be helpful. A team charter is the team's social contract. Issues that are important to a team charter include team values (pace and hours expected), working agreements, ground rules, and group norms (PMI 2017b).

Sprint or iteration. In scrum, an agile method, the time-boxed iterations are called sprints (Schwaber and Sutherland 2017). The length of a sprint is designated at the start and is as short as a week or as long as a month. The project becomes a series of sprints. See Figure 7.7 for a graphic representation of the agile lifecycle. The project and team charters, as well as the final review or lessons learned, are assumed to bracket the agile lifecycle and are not shown in the figure.

Product backlog. Backlog is a name given to the "ordered list of user-centric requirements that a team maintains for a product" (PMI 2017b). The backlog is similar to the WBS, in that it helps scope the work. However, the backlog does not start as a complete list of all deliverables. The list is prioritized, evolves, and is managed throughout the project. And, the backlog increments try to express the value the project is seeking by describing a user story. For example, "As a market researcher,

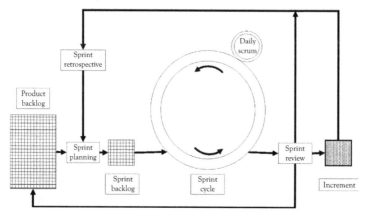

Figure 7.7 The agile lifecycle (adapted from Schwaber and Sutherland 2017)

I want to document the buyer demographics, so that our client better understands the customer" (Louie 2005).

Sprint backlog. These are the increments from the product backlog that are selected to be produced as a final product during a sprint or iteration. The current sprint is always working on the highest priority product backlog increments that have yet to be completed. The number of increments in the sprint backlog is limited to the number of increments the team can complete during the allotted time.

Retrospectives and planning. The term retrospective is used very broadly here to represent at least five different events in the agile process. The daily scrum is a short daily meeting in which yesterday's work is reviewed, today's work is announced, and any impediments to work are discussed. After each sprint, the backlog and increments completed are reviewed for their relevance to adding value. This is called a sprint review. Also, after each sprint, the team's work process is reviewed, and suggestions made for the team's improvement. This is indicated in Figure 7.7 as the sprint retrospective. Before a sprint ends, a sprint planning session is held to determine the next sprint backlog. And, finally, at the end of the project, an overall review is conducted to promote continuous improvement (PMI 2017b; Schwaber and Sutherland 2017). Communication with the project sponsor in the agile or adaptive approach is more engaged and more frequent than in the predictive model. The teams are expected to be self-directed with team members dedicated 100 percent to the project. Leadership is more facilitative than managerial (PMI 2017b).

Implications

So, what does this mean for the student project? First, everyone in the project team needs to be aware of all this, and they all need to commit to practicing the processes. If anyone is unfamiliar with the process model or has doubts, they must be brought into alignment with the rest of the team and meet consensus. This is particularly true on agile projects. Take the time up front, even if there is pressure to start working. If class meets on a weekly basis, then commit to weekly sprints. Whatever is finished during that sprint should be as close to a final product as the team can envision. For example, and in keeping with the business case mentioned previously, if the business, stakeholders, and solutions requirements drafts are part of the weekly sprint backlog, then by the end of the week, the drafts should be ready in a form that closely approximates what is expected as the final product. Make sure the arguments are logical and founded on facts. Synthesize the disparate information in an easy-to-understand narrative. Make sure grammar is correct, sources are correctly cited, and the product complies with any other criteria set out by the instructor or project sponsor. During the week, do not be afraid to contact the sponsor or instructor for clarification. In an agile environment, everyone is considered to be available and aware of their obligations to the project and its processes. Every day, the scrum master or project manager needs to convene a quick meeting at which everyone must be present, in person or virtually. The three questions (aforementioned) are asked of each team member. The team and scrum master help out where they are needed to.

About two days before the end of the sprint, plan the backlog for the next week's sprint. At the end of the sprint, review the work done and the team performance. If changes need to be made, then incorporate them into the next sprint. As work progresses, the team will become aware of what kind of workload or pace is sustainable. The backlog is adjusted accordingly and communicated with the project sponsor. Schedule increments in the backlog that coincide with required in-progress deliverables such as status reports, drafts, or prototypes. The key for the whole team, and the responsibility of the scrum master, is to maintain a disciplined process.

Conclusion

This chapter covered projects that contribute to practice. These projects are characterized by having a real or made-up customer and are, in general terms, aligned with the regulative cycle that was presented in Chapter 6. Whenever undertaking a project for a client, the team must first of all understand the business case well enough to determine a project approach. The approach taken toward the project can be different depending on the environment, as was discussed in Chapter 3. Whether the project is approached by predicting a well thought-out lifecycle or electing to approach the project as an evolving set of requirements, the team must adopt the appropriate project processes to assure success. The chapter showed the five different basic processes, that is, initiate, plan, execute, monitor and control, and closing, and provided practical advice. Additional information was provided on the agile approach.

Due to the involvement of a client, there is a lot of emphasis on managing and communicating with the client. Examples of documents and forms were provided. It was also noted that a disciplined approach is the best way to account for all the variables that exist in the project environment, and that these variables should be identified from the theories, models, techniques, and methods that are part of the course environment. Furthermore, the approaches covered in this chapter are not only the best way to approach a school project for a client, but they also represent the approaches that graduates can use to build a career in a professional setting.

CHAPTER 8

Projects that Contribute to Theory

As was explained in Chapter 6, projects that contribute to theory generally follow the empirical cycle, although they may start at different spots in this cycle. This chapter provides insights into how to conduct a project that contributes to theory, and for ease of the discussion, the general part of the end result of this type of project, typically a research paper, is described. Although this exact format is not always appropriate and although the project is typically iterative so that these parts in a paper are not linearly developed, this setup is followed here for ease of the discussion. Thus, the following areas are covered: abstract, introduction, purpose and research questions, literature review, conceptual framework, methodology, data, discussion, and conclusion sections, and the reflection. The chapter ends with conclusions.

Abstract Section

The abstract is typically written once the research project is completed. It is at that stage that the content of the final product, that is, the research paper is known, and thus what needs to be written for the abstract.

Purpose

The purpose of the abstract is to summarize the article so that interested readers can quickly get a sense of the research project.

Approach

The abstract is, as the word indicates, an abstract of the rest of the article. This means that it essentially should summarize the article by discussing a little of each section. Therefore, it typically contains something from the introduction section (why is the topic important), the research purpose and research questions, methodology, findings, and conclusions.

Implications and Practical Tips

A good way to write an abstract is to look at each major section of the research paper and determine the main message in one or two sentences. Combining all these sentences and writing it coherently will lead to suitable abstract. The main mistake found with student research projects is that many students write an introduction instead of an abstract. This is often the result of (a) starting the abstract early in the research project or (b) not finishing the abstract after the paper has been written. As a consequence, it may contain sentences that are written in terms of plans versus what was accomplished or, for example, only describe the motive for the research without describing the findings.

Example

The course theme for a theory-oriented project was identified as technology and economic development. Within this theme, student teams had freedom to define their own project focus. One group decided to do research on the role of high-speed broadband communication networks and their impact on GDP per capita. The abstract for their final research paper consisted of the following.

> The purpose of this paper is to gain insight into the importance of fast and efficient communications in terms of broadband communication. The question is: how does broadband communication affect gross domestic product (GDP) per capita? The design method utilized data from 142 countries using both static and time-series analysis techniques. The data was analyzed to investigate the effects of broadband communications on GDP. The time series included a period of approximately 10 years concurrent with economic expansion for the selected countries. A strong correlation between the availability of high-speed broadband

communications capability and economic growth was discovered. The correlation supports the idea that, if countries want to experience significant economic growth, they should invest in broadband communications infrastructure.

This example illustrates several key elements of the abstract. This abstract clearly communicates what the research project was about. It also contains elements of the methodology by explaining that it involved 142 countries and static and time-series analysis. It also shares the main findings and the implications of those findings.

Other items that are often found and could have been included in this abstract are: why the research is important, what the limitations of the project were (typically in terms of methodology and what that means for the ability to draw conclusions), and suggestions for further research.

Introduction Section

The introduction section is typically something that gets written more toward the end of the project, although it gets developed over time. As the student team gets more expertise in the topic area that is being investigated, they are better able to articulate what the project is about.

Purpose

The purpose of the introduction section of a research paper is to introduce the topic and to entice the reader to read more. Note that this is different than for a project that contributes to practice such as a business report where results are typically presented first and explanations follow.

Approach

The introduction section has more flexibility than the rest of the research paper in terms of the content. As its main purpose is to explain the relevance of the topic, it is permissible to use popular media. For instance, the popular media may provide numbers such as quantities or percentages that indicate how important a topic is. For example, the size of a market. Of course, when this media is used, it should be cited and referenced appropriately. A fun part of the introduction is, therefore, to search for all kinds of information that provide an indication of why the topic is important. In other words, in terms of (critical) thinking skills, the emphasis is on searching for interesting information that can help to explain the importance of the topic.

Implications and Practical Tips

The skills required to write a good introduction section are general writing skills and the ability to write in an enticing manner. Additionally, the student team will need basic search skills so that they can find information related to the topic, which expresses the importance of the topic or the need for research on the topic. A practical tip is to read as much as possible, and to start early with this reading. Reading a lot early on gives exposure to the topic area, which will give a broad sense of the topic area overall. Furthermore, this early exposure, if it includes scientific literature, can help with forming initial ideas on the focus of the research project. Because it is important in projects to indicate where information is coming from (citing and referencing), it is recommended to keep track of what you read and include referencing information. This can, for example, be accomplished by creating a standard form that states the referencing information and a short description of the content of the document.

Example

The course theme for a project was identified as economic development. Within this theme, student teams had freedom to define their own project focus. One group decided to do research on natural disasters and how international financial aid related to natural disasters could influence a developing economy. For the final research paper, the group had the following introduction:

On Tuesday, January 12, 2010, at 4:53 p.m., a 7.0 magnitude earthquake struck 15 miles west, south-west of Port-au-Prince, Haiti (Daniell 2011). The quake struck without warning, catching

Haiti completely unprepared. The country had little to no seis-mic-resistant construction in place, and many underlying politi-cal and socioeconomic problems (Daniell 2011). The earthquake claimed the lives of between 92,000 and 225,000 Haitians; over 300,000 were injured; and 1, 850,000 were left homeless (Daniell 2011). In the months that followed, 1,200,000 people were left huddled, sick, and destitute in homeless shelters around Port-Au-Prince; another 150,000 moved overseas, and 500,000 spread out across Haiti (Daniell 2011). Estimates place the total economic loss between $7.5 and $8.5 billion (Daniell 2011).

Large sudden natural disasters, such as Haiti's 2010 earthquake, generate destruction on a massive scale; capture widespread media attention; and increase the public's awareness of the destructive nature of natural disasters. But, what if natural disasters were not entirely a bad thing? Since 1969, numerous empirical studies have been conducted on this very question, and today, there is a small but growing consensus that natural disasters do, in fact, benefit the economic condition of an impacted region. This is the so-called *growth* model.

At the same time, the academic research into the consequences of natural disasters remain fairly limited, with a great of that lit-erature focused on their short-term benefits. To our knowledge, there have only been a handful of studies into the long-term con-sequences of natural disasters. What is more, these studies fail to fully develop or answer why natural disasters impact the long-term economic condition of a country. In this paper, we contrib-ute to the discussion of the long-run impact of natural disasters on gross domestic output by examining the impact of large natural disasters on the foundations of economic growth.

This example demonstrates several important characteristics. First, the authors demonstrate the importance of the topic by explaining the size of the impact in terms of dollars and human lives affected. Second, they briefly explain what has already been researched. Third, they then explain what they are going to do in their research project and how this is different. Last, but not least, they appropriately cite and reference so that their opinion is removed and instead it relies on information from others, and because of the appropriate citing, readers can check this information. Note that there are many citations. Every time something is stated that comes from another source, the student team identified this.

Purpose and Research Questions

Every project, including projects that contribute to theory, must have a purpose. In projects that contribute to theory, the purpose is roughly *contributing to the existing theory on....* The purpose should be clearly stated and distinct from the research questions that are posed in the project. Normally, the purpose is contributing to theory, which then leads to a question that relates to that contribution. This is the central research question. The central research question is often a somewhat *bigger* question that then gets logically divided into smaller research questions. The answers to the research questions exactly answer the central research question, no more and no less.

Purpose

The purpose of the purpose statement and research questions is to communicate to the reader why the research project took place. That means what knowledge was sought, and related to this, what research questions were posed.

Approach

The research purpose and research questions can be somewhat complicated because, in course research projects, they get refined over time. The problem is that, when a course research project is started, there is often not sufficient information available to determine the exact research purpose and questions. As the student team becomes more knowledgeable in the topic area, they are able to adjust their research purpose and questions over time. The formulation of the research purpose and research questions is, therefore, very much iteratively developed, see Chapter 6 and Figure 6.4.

Another complicating factor is the placing of the research purpose and research questions within the article. The research purpose should appear after an argument, that is, justification, has been established for the need for research. The research questions follow this.

Following this, there needs to be logical reasoning about how this central research question is logically divided into smaller research questions. So, having a central research question and following this immediately having a list of four research questions is not a good approach because the logic and reasoning are missing.

There are two logical spots for the research purpose and research questions. This can be either at the end of the introduction section when the importance of the topic has been explained and if the introduction also explains the theoretical motive for need for the research project, that is, that there is a gap in knowledge. Or, it is at the end of the literature review when typically as a result of an analysis of the existing literature, it has become clear what the gap in the existing knowledge is and why research is necessary and on what exactly.

Implications and Practical Tips

The conundrum of the research purpose and research questions is that the exact formulation isn't known in advance. This relates to the iterative nature of the project as discussed in Chapter 6. Thus, at the beginning of the research project, there is not a well-defined research purpose and research questions, which means that there is little direction in what to do. Consequently, a student team simply has to come up with something so that a direction is formulated and the research project can be started, but also with keeping in mind that it will change over time as the student team becomes more knowledgeable.

Example

The course theme for a research project was identified as global developments in additive manufacturing, that is, 3D printing. Within this theme, student teams had freedom to define their own project focus. One group decided to do research on the medical applications of 3D printing.

To keep the research projects on track in the course, the overall project was divided into three phases. At the end of each phase, the student teams had to report, that means submit the research paper under development, as well as present on the progress. The three phases were (1) introduction with research questions, (2) literature review with conceptual framework, and (3) the final phase that completed the project and included the methodology, collecting of data, and drawing conclusions.

At the end of the first, that is, introduction phase and formulating research questions, the student team came up with the following:

With the project, the issues addressed will pertain to the utilization of 3D printers in creating organs. Currently, the questions to be investigated are:

- How does additive manufacturing relate to stem cell research?
- Is producing 3D printed organs a long-term solution to patient health concerns?
- What obstacles will be present for the body to accept the 3D-manufactured organ?
- Are there limitations or strengths that a 3D printed organ can have in comparison to natural organs?
- Can a single printer make multiple types of organs?
- What is the demand for organs around the world?
- What will be the price and ownership of these available organs if or when implementation takes place?
- What will be the social and cultural acceptance for these organs?

This list is not all inclusive, as we expect our research to lead us toward a variety of new inquiries.

At the end of the second phase, that is, the literature review and the development of the conceptual model, when more insight was gained into 3D printing in the medical field, the team changed this to:

The following research will seek to explore the viability of 3D printing as a way to combat the scarcity of organs for transplant. The following research questions were posed:

1. How is the need for organs determined by societal factors? Specifically, economic factors, political factors, and underlying culture.
2. Is a country's attitude toward incentivizing organ donation related to their respective supply and demand curve of organs for transplant?
3. If strong cultural attitudes are shown to be significant, will these attitudes correlate to the potential for adoption of bioprinting as a solution to the issue of low supply, high demand of organs for transplant?

At the end of the third phase, that is, the completion of the research project, the team had changed the purpose and research questions to:

The purpose of this exploratory research is to explain whether socioeconomic factors influence the global diffusion of a medical technology and what correlation (if any) exists among these factors and the global diffusion of a medical technology. As part of the literature review, the team identified four socioeconomic factors as significant variables. Based on this, the following research questions were then identified:

1. Does a correlation exist among socioeconomic factors and the global adoption of a medical technology?
2. Will bioprinting of organs follow a diffusion pattern similar to other medical technologies and their global adoption?

This example illustrates the iterative nature of the research project. In the first phase of the project, when the student team had limited knowledge of the area under investigation, the research purpose is relatively general, that is, study 3D printing of organs, and there is a large set of research questions that reflect the many questions the student team came up with to look into. After the literature review was completed, the student team became more focused. The purpose related to determining viability of 3D printing of organs to deal with a societal problem, and the research questions were reduced to a question related to the need for organs, a question related to the donation of organs, and only the last question was 3D printing specific. At the end of the project, when the students had the most knowledge about the topic area, the direction had changed quite a bit. The purpose changed to one that had a focus on the (global) diffusion of a (medical) technology. There were two research questions where the first looked at the relationship between socioeconomic variables and diffusion of medical technology in general.[1] The second question then compared this with the specific socioeconomic circumstances of bioprinting to get an idea whether bioprinting is likely to follow the same diffusion path as previous medical technologies.

Literature Review Section

After the introduction section comes the literature review section. The literature review section has much less flexibility in terms of what should be covered. The literature should be focused on an analysis of previous research. Therefore, it should mainly contain citations and references to scholarly articles and not popular press articles.

Purpose

The primary purpose of the literature review is to identify a gap in the existing knowledge, which is subsequently addressed in the research study. A secondary purpose is to demonstrate knowledge and understanding of previous studies that have taken place in the field of interest. For the literature review, the key is to conduct an analysis of the existing studies in the field so that an area can be identified, which, for *theoretical* reasons, needs further research. This can be because previous research has ignored a specific scope or niche, or because previous research has led to conflicting findings. The former is challenging to point out because, if researchers are unable to find a study with a particular scope, then this could also mean that they didn't do an adequate search. The latter typically means that there are other, as yet unidentified, variables that play a role

---

[1] The team compared the influence of socioeconomic variables on the global diffusion patterns of in-vitro fertilization (IVF), polio vaccines, occurrence of stem cell research, and use of condoms.

in explaining the phenomenon. For example, a 2016 article in *Industry Week*[2] showed that two independent consulting companies had both done a study on reshoring.[3] While the A.T. Kearney group concluded, based on their data, that reshoring may be over before it began and that reshoring failed to keep up with offshoring,[4] the Boston Consulting Group concluded, based on their data, that reshoring is increasing and that reshoring increased by 250 percent since 2012. These conflicting findings about the same phenomenon indicate that there might be additional variables that play a role, and connected to this, that there may have been differences in the measurements, that is, the methodology.[5]

Approach

The literature review is a challenging aspect for graduate students as well as for experienced researchers. The literature review requires critically thinking about previously published research studies and is essentially *a search for variables*. This search for variables results in the conceptual framework.

The most commonly made mistake with the literature review is that authors end up describing the existing literature instead of analyzing the literature. One reason for this is that, when a student team delves into a new topic, they first need to develop an understanding of that topic. Hence, they typically end up describing the literature. However, describing or summing up the literature is at best at level two in Bloom's taxonomy, that is, understand; See Chapter 2, for example Table 2.3. What is required for a graduate-level research project is that previous

---

[2] http://industryweek.com/global-economy/reshoring-increasing-or-declining

[3] Reshoring is a situation where companies move previously offshored production back to the domestic location.

[4] Offshoring is a situation where companies move production to other nations. One reason why this may occur is due to expected lower production cost.

[5] In the example, the Boston Consulting Group data comes from an annual online survey of senior-level U.S.-based manufacturing executives, whereas the A.T. Kearney study looked at trends in the manufacturing import ratio from 14 Asian markets. The import ratio is defined as the imports of manufactured goods divided by the U.S. domestic gross output of manufactured goods.

studies are analyzed (level 4) and evaluated (level 5) so that a logical and theoretical argument can be presented that justifies why the research project should be undertaken.

Another common error with the literature review, and somewhat exacerbated by the previously conducted search for the introduction section, is that researchers have gotten an idea of the availability of data. With that, researchers often start to explore the data further to look at relationships. As a consequence, the research project might more or less skip the literature review portion and move to the fascinating data analysis part. This is a critical mistake. First, it may lead to reinventing the wheel as these analysis may simply lead to conclusions that are already discussed in the literature, but that the researchers are not (yet) aware of. Second, it is often extremely difficult, if not impossible, to write-up a literature review after the study has been done that is still consistent and is able to demonstrate a theoretical justification for why the study needed to take place.

Searching for literature can happen in at least three ways. First, a general search can take place, for instance, by using keywords in academic databases. What should be kept in mind here is that it is often necessary to use different types of terms. For example, when looking for reshoring, another term that is similar is backshoring. Searching for outsourcing or offshoring might also lead to relevant literature. Second, once a source is found, then analyzing the list of references in that source can lead to additional articles. Note that these articles, because they were in the reference list, are older. The third approach is a cited reference search. In this instance, once a source is found, then a cited reference search leads to publications that have references to this source. In other words, it is similar to the second type, but instead of going backward in time, it goes forward in time.

Implications and Practical Tips

The literature review should be considered as *a search for variables*. Within the topic area chosen by the student team, they need to find out what others studies have done. This means, looking at what relationships have been investigated previously, what was found about those relationships, and in particular, how were the variables defined and measured. Especially, using techniques such as comparing and contrasting findings and their measurements can be helpful. Related to this is the system of sorting. Sorting might work best with hard copies instead of electronic copies of articles. The idea is that articles that have been found and read get sorted into different piles. In order to do this, it is necessary to compare and contrast the content of different articles and to determine or discover what is similar or different. With only a few articles, they all will appear to deal with the same issue, that is, the main topic of the research project. But, as more literature is found and processed, the pile of articles should be split. This forces the team to think about what the articles in each pile have in common, while at the same time forcing them to think about what is different between the different piles. For example, a research project on the topic of international technology transfer can very quickly lead to many results. A simple search on Google Scholar on the terms *international technology transfer* leads to more than four million results. However, once a team delves into these articles, different categories of articles can be found. For example, some articles may present descriptions of cases. Some may deal with specific aspects such as how the technology was transferred. Some may be dealing with constraints on technology transfer, for example, international property rights. Some articles may be about the management of the transfer process, while others may be more about the technology, and so forth. Comparing, contrasting, and sorting these articles in meaningful piles enhances the ability to discover the most important variables, while at the same time, it provides the team with ideas on how these variables have been measured in previous academic studies.

Especially in the beginning of the research project, the literature review has more emphasis on learning about the field and using this information to refine the research purpose and research questions when it leads to increased insight about the potential gap in knowledge. One thing to pay attention to during the literature review is to spend time wisely. An analogy is a target as shown in Figure 8.1. If the purpose

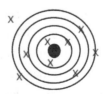

Figure 8.1 The target of the literature review

and research questions for the research are the bull's eye, then (a) there shouldn't be literature on that bull's eye, as in that case, the study has already been done and (b) most time and effort should be spent on the inner circles of the target. Many student teams spend too much time on reading and analyzing articles that they find, but that are more toward the outside of the target. This is not an efficient use of time. Not making adequate distinctions between what is important and what is less relevant can easily lead to becoming overwhelmed with the project. Article titles can often be misleading and may provide limited indication of how useful an article is for the literature review. Reading the abstracts of the articles, on the other hand, can quickly provide a sense of the value of an article and how closely aligned it is with the research purpose and research questions.

In general, a team should expect to have to find at least 40 articles for a semester-long project that contributes to theory. Not all of these will be relevant for the literature review that will eventually be presented in the research paper and final presentation. However, some papers will be needed to develop initial thinking on the topic. Due to the iterative nature of the research project, at later stages in the project, the literature review section often needs to be trimmed. This requires tough decisions because of the amount of time and effort that has gone into previous developments and writing, but inevitably, some of the literature that was consulted earlier will end up being misaligned with a continuously refined research topic.

An Example of a Literature Review is Provided in Appendix I

The literature review example in Appendix I fulfills the primary purpose of identifying a gap in the existing knowledge. In fact, a few paragraphs above the statement of the hypotheses, it explicitly mentions this gap. Additionally, in particular, in the section *banking adoption,* but also in the section *culture and business,* the literature review is not just a repeat, that is, a description of previous studies, but rather it contains an analysis that includes a comparison of previous findings. It is based on an evaluation of these findings that conclusions are drawn about the theoretical reasons why more research is necessary and what should be studied. This led to the hypotheses.

This literature review also fulfills the secondary purpose, that means, it demonstrates knowledge and understanding of previous studies that have taken place on the adoption of banking, that is, having a bank account. While the literature review does not discuss a lot of studies that are closely related to the field under investigation, the breadth of topics covered, such as the section on culture, demonstrates that the authors have knowledge about the field.

The Conceptual Framework

The conceptual framework is a logical extension of the literature review. While the literature review leads to the identification of the gap in the existing knowledge, and thus the variables and relationships that will be studied in the project, this is summarized in the conceptual framework and depicted with a graph.

Purpose

The purpose of the conceptual framework is to show and discuss which variables and relationships will be studied in the project.

Approach

Many research articles that are published in academic journals have a qualitative discussion of the conceptual framework. Studies that take place in the realm of the natural sciences orientation are more likely to have a graphical depiction of the conceptual framework than those coming from a social sciences, that is, interpretivist orientation. Nevertheless, because a primary purpose of the research project is to develop critical thinking, it is advisable to make a graphical representation. If a team has difficulty making a graph that shows the variables and their relationships that will be studied, then this is often an indication that they have not developed a sufficient level of comprehension of their chosen topic area. Also, if the conceptual framework is not clear, then the next step, that is, determining the methodology, cannot be taken because without knowing which variables and relationships will be examined, it is not meaningful to discuss how they will exactly be measured and where data will be collected from.

Implications and Practical Tips

The conceptual framework should be logically aligned with the research purpose, research questions, and literature review. This means that the variables and relationships should be logically connected to, and come from, the conclusions from the literature review.

Two common mistakes occur with the conceptual framework. First, there is no conceptual framework. This is because the team has not progressed enough and has not really *mastered* or understood what others have studied in terms of variables and relationships and has not been able to identify a gap, and with it, logically, the variables and relationships that should be studied in the project.

The second common mistake is that the conceptual framework is not aligned with the literature review. This can occur when the team splits up the tasks of the research project and does not communicate sufficiently about this; see also the discussion in Chapter 5. As a result, one person may be responsible for writing the literature review section, while another person may be responsible for writing the conceptual framework section, and without proper communication between them. there is a high probability that a misalignment will occur.

To develop a good conceptual framework requires that first, a sufficient amount of literature has been included in the literature review. Not reading enough literature, often occurring due to procrastination or underestimating the time required early on in the project, leads to insufficient understanding of the topic area. Second, in order to determine variables and relationships, the literature has to be *analyzed* so that it becomes clear what variables and relationships others have studied and how they have done so. Third, by comparing and contrasting, and sorting the articles, see the discussion on the literature review, the gap should become clear, and this leads to the proper identification of variables. Making a graph is relatively simple if it is understood which variables are expected to influence what.

Example

The course theme for a research project was additive manufacturing. One student team decided to do research on the adoption of consumer-level

3D printers. As the main topic was that of adoption of a technology, the literature review was focused on finding variables from previous studies that determine whether a technology gets adopted. Based on the discussion of several technology diffusion theories, the team identified three important constructs: prior conditions, knowledge, and persuasion. The team also found that some variables influence these constructs: felt needs or problems, the norms of the social system, income, education, complexity of the technology, and the relative advantage of the technology. Together, these constructs and mediating variables were expected to influence the adoption of a technology in general, and this was going to be studied in the specific instance of consumer 3D printers. Based on this, the team presented the following graphical representation of their conceptual framework; see Figure 8.2.

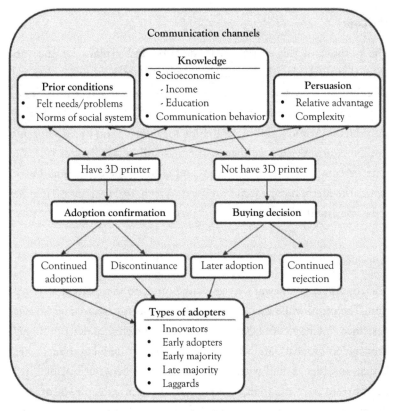

Figure 8.2 Example of a conceptual framework

This example of a conceptual framework illustrates how the team had a good comprehension of the existing literature or theories on the adoption of a technology. The newness in this regard was the combination of concepts from different models and the application of this in a new setting, that is, the situation of consumers adopting 3D printers. The conceptual framework identified the variables that the team was going to measure to be able to explain why people adopted the technology, or why they did not.

Methodology Section

The methodology is the most *technical* section of the paper. For this part of the research project, it is important to understand the different research approaches that were explained in Chapter 6.

Purpose

The purpose of this section is to describe and explain for the variables that were identified in the conceptual framework what data will be collected how, and from where. This part of the paper provides an opportunity for further development of critical thinking skills. For the introduction section, skills in searching for information were important. The literature review was theory-oriented and allows project teams to practice comparing and contrasting and creating the conceptual framework. The methodology section relies on a technical description that has to be consistent.

Approach

The conceptual framework serves as the input to the methodology section. The team, while keeping in mind the different research approaches described in Chapter 6, has to come up with a technical description and explanation of what data will be collected. The underlying thought here is that, in order to find patterns in relationships between variables, it is necessary to have variation in these variables. For example, in order to investigate whether the world price of oil is correlated to the world price of sugar,[6] it is necessary to have data that includes varying levels of oil and sugar prices.

Implications and Practical Tips ˙

One of the challenges of the methodology section is not having a sufficiently developed conceptual framework. Without a clear conceptual framework, there is no point in moving forward with a methodology section. The main point of the methodology section is to explain how *all* variables are defined and measured, how data will be collected and from where, how the data will be analyzed, and how this will lead to meaningful results. The most common mistakes made by student teams in terms of the methodology are that it does not clearly define the variables, doesn't explain how they will be measured, and very important, it does not have sufficient variation of data points so that conclusions cannot be reached.

An Example of a Methodology Discussion Is Provided in Appendix J

What this example shows is a thought-out plan for data collection. The data will be collected by means of a survey, and the rationale for using a survey is provided. It has also been explained who will be approached for participating in the survey and the reasons behind this selection. Furthermore, it is explained how the survey will be distributed and how many surveys need to be gathered for meaningful results. For each of the variables, it has been explained how the variable is measured in the survey, that is, what questions are asked.

Data, Discussion, and Conclusion Sections

Once the methodology section has been completed, the rest of the paper is more or less an implementation of the plan for data collection. After

---

[6] It does. This is because Brazil is a major player in the world sugar market, but at a certain level of oil prices, it is beneficial for Brazil to use sugar for the production of ethanol as an alternative for fuel. This affects the availability of sugar in the world.

the data has been collected, it needs to be presented, then patterns and findings need to be discussed, and conclusions need to be drawn.

Purpose

The purpose of the data and discussion sections is that the findings from the study are shared. Especially in studies with a natural science orientation, the data is typically separated from the discussion. For studies with a social science orientation, for example, a case study, this is more difficult to accomplish. When data and discussion are separated, then the purpose of the data section is to share the *raw* data with the reader so that the reader can form his or her own opinion about what was found. Note that there is a difference in communication for projects that contribute to practice and those that contribute to theory. For the former, it is typical to present the conclusions first and explain how they were reached later. For the latter, it is typical to let the reader come to his or her own conclusions; therefore, conclusions are presented last. See also Chapter 9. The discussion section is where the analysis of the data takes place and where the findings are compared with the findings from earlier studies. That means, it is connected back to the literature review.

Approach

Once the methodology has been determined, then the collection of data is more or less straightforward, that is, it is simply following the plan. Once the data is collected, then the data will have to be analyzed. This often involves determining correlations (studies with natural science orientation) or interpretations (studies with social science orientation; this may involve interpretations about causality). This is connected back to the literature review, and therefore requires similar activities in terms of critical thinking: comparing and contrasting the findings of the project with those of previous studies.

Implications and Practical Tips

The main advice for data, discussion, and conclusion is to be aware of and correctly apply statistical tests for quantitative studies and to provide enough descriptions and details for studies that have a more qualitative orientation. Keep in mind that projects in classroom situations are oriented on a learning element so that instructors know that it is not always possible to collect enough data to have meaningful statistical analysis. However, incorrectly applying statistical tools or applying incorrect statistical tools are major concerns and demonstrate a lack of insight. If there is not enough data to do a meaningful analysis, then it is better to state this rather than to ignore it and continue with a statistical analysis, which can't technically be applied due to a lack of data. Note also that, for example, describing average is not always meaningful. It can be applied for interval and ratio scales, but not to nominal or ordinal scales.

Example

A research project was conducted with the purpose of looking at economic growth. The specific focus was on the role of R&D. During the literature review, the student team discussed academic studies that investigated the link between R&D activities and technological and economic progress. Based on this, the team developed a conceptual model that included variables such as the level of development of a nation, the population size, the human development index, and the GDP. All of these were expected to influence the amount of money that a nation invests in R&D activities. In the methodology section, the student team explained that it would collect data based on varying levels of economic development (factor-driven, efficiency-driven, or innovation-driven), as well as size of the country (small, medium, and large),[7] leading to nine groups of countries. For each group, three countries were selected so that for each stage of economic development, there were nine countries. The final selection of countries that were included in the study is shown in Table 8.1.

The team also described in the methodology section that it would use secondary sources for its data such as from, for instance, the World Bank. The data that was collected was put into a spreadsheet and was used for various analysis. While the complete spreadsheet was not included in

---

[7] These categories were defined by the student team so that it was clear what was part of which group. For example, the team defined large countries as those with populations of 80 million or more.

Table 8.1 Sample for the study

	Stage 1: Factor-driven			Stage 2: Efficiency-driven			Stage 3: Innovation-driven		
	Small	Medium	Large	Small	Medium	Large	Small	Medium	Large
	Burkina Faso	Cote d'Ivoire	India	Georgia	Morocco	China	Norway	France	United States
	Malawi	Ethiopia	Pakistan	Salvador	South Africa	Brazil	Singapore	South Korea	Japan
	Liberia	Mali	Mali	Bulgaria	Ukraine	Russia	Austria	United Kingdom	Germany

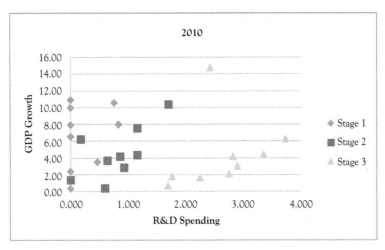

Figure 8.3 GDP growth and R&D spending

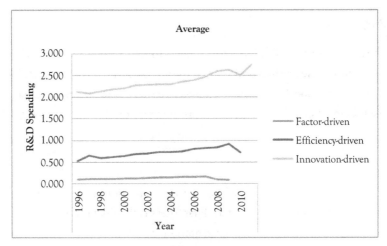

Figure 8.4 R&D spending by year

the research report, the team selected some of the data to share the data section in the form of figures, see for example Figures 8.3 and 8.4. Some of these are shown as follows.

This example shows how a team collected quantitative data from secondary sources. This data was combined into a spreadsheet, which subsequently allowed the team to conduct analysis and look for correlations between variables. The data was displayed in the form of figures in the research paper, which allows readers to form their own opinion.

Appendix K provides an example of a conclusion and discussion section. This example shows how, based on data, conclusions are drawn. As indicated earlier, one of the main reasons for research projects in a graduate program isn't necessarily the outcome of the research project, but more the process, and with it, the development of critical thinking. This is, for example, demonstrated in the limitation paragraph and insights that can be used for more research.

The Reflection

The reflection is not a part of the outcome of the research project, that is, the research paper. However, it is an important part of the overall process, and therefore may be a required component of a classroom project.

Purpose

The purpose of the reflection is for students to reflect upon the process followed during the research project. This means, taking a step back and evaluate what was done, how well it was done, determine how things could have been done differently, and overall determining lessons for improvement.

Approach

There is no prescribed approach to writing a reflection, but there are several topics that should be covered. First, there is the final product, that is, the research report, article, or presentation. Second, there is the process, that is, what was done, how, in what order, and so forth. Third, there is the thinking about recommendations for improvement.

Implications and Practical Tips

As stated earlier in this chapter, the goal of a research project in a graduate business course isn't so much the outcome, but rather, the process of the project. Therefore, the main emphasis in the reflection should be on what was learned about that process. This includes struggles with methodological uncertainty and requirements uncertainty, see Chapter 3, for example

Figure 3.2. It also includes dealing with topic vagueness, strategies for searching for scientific articles use of the library and getting help from the university librarians, how critical thinking skills were applied or enhanced due to the project, and so on.

Example

An example is provided in Appendix L. This example shows the conscious reflection upon the research project by a student team. It describes what the students have learned about the process of doing a research project. It explains, for instance, the difficulties in determining the research direction and specific focus, the selection of the variables, the iterative nature of the project, and contains advice for future research projects. Overall, this reflection demonstrates a high level of awareness and learning.

Conclusion

This chapter provided insight into how teams can conduct projects that contribute to theory. These type of projects have more emphasis on theoretical reasoning than projects that contribute to practice. The main portions of the outcome of the project, that is, a research paper or presentation, were discussed. Nevertheless, it should be noted that not all papers end up with this exact format, and that the development takes place iteratively over time.

One of the advantages of projects that contribute to theory is that the sections of the final product have very distinct characteristics. For example, the methodology is the technical section of the paper. Nevertheless, sometimes students get confused. A common confusion is where students end up mixing data and the literature review. This is understandable when secondary data is used for the study, and because this comes from the literature, things can become confusing. The thing to keep in mind is that the literature review is a theoretical discussion that is focused on searching for variables. The data section is about sharing data, quantitative or qualitative, that was collected in an effort to answer questions. Another critical mistake that was discussed in this chapter is where a team starts to work from the perspective of the available data. This almost never leads to an outcome that has a new contribution to theory, and it is extremely difficult if not impossible to correct late in the project. In some instances, it may mean that a team will have to start again, almost from scratch.

Projects that contribute to theory can be implemented differently by different instructors. For example, some instructors may provide the assignment and require only one document, that is, the final paper at the end of the academic turn. Others may want to put *milestones* into place to make sure that students keep on track. In some situations, instructors will provide a lot of guidance and direction, see the task project in Chapter 4, while others instructors may give the student team more responsibility, see the problem project in Chapter 4.

As a final comment, if student projects that contribute to theory and that involve humans (for example, through surveys) are planned to be submitted to academic outlets, then universities typically require the completion of an IRB process. If it is only part of the classroom experience, that is, there is no plan for submission to, for example, a journal, then some universities don't require it, while other universities may also require it in that situation. Thus, a team should make itself aware of the regulations at their university and plan accordingly. For example, to complete the IRB process takes time. In some instances, it will mean that a survey may be designed, but not distributed. This may still be acceptable for the course instructor as long as the critical thinking underlying the design of the survey and the combination with the literature review are of high quality.

CHAPTER 9

Communicating Project Results

The final result of a project is often a written product that frequently has to be presented as well. The key issue to keep in mind for any communication, whether written or oral, is to appropriately target the audience. This requires an in-depth understanding of the purpose of the project and its final outcome. It also requires an in-depth understanding of who will read the result of the project and who will be in the audience when the results are presented. The following discussion is divided into a discussion of written and oral communication before reaching conclusions at the end of the chapter.

Chapter 4 distinguished the two major categories of projects: projects that contribute to practice and projects that contribute to theory. Chapters 7 and 8 provided more insight into those two main categories. Chapters 7 and 8 also already provided examples of writing. For example, due to the importance of clients in the projects that contribute to practice, many forms of reporting to the client during the project were shared in Chapter 7.

Reports for Projects that Contribute to Practice

As was discussed in Chapter 4, projects that contribute to practice can fall into several different categories, such as task, discipline, or problem project. Although this distinction influences how the project is conducted and how much direction is provided by the course instructor, this distinction does not make a difference in terms of writing the report. Similarly, even though some projects are discovery-oriented, while others are utilization-oriented, this distinction does not influence the writing of the report.

There is extensive literature on writing (business) reports. For instance, sources such as Adefolarin (2015), Clark and Clark (2016),

Daniel (2013), Flood (2008), Garner (2013), Greenhall (2010), and Holden (2011) can provide valuable insight into how to write a report. Note that most of these sources also have their weaknesses. For example, they may or may not discuss the importance of citing and referencing and the need to look for multiple sources. Some books emphasize the importance of data, while others may focus more on spelling and grammar issues et cetera.

The following discussion is based on some of the ideas presented by Daniel (2012) and focuses on (a) the purpose of the project, (b) the target audience, (c) the structure of the report, (d) the role of theory, and citing and references, (e) formatting guidelines, (f) the role of graphs and figures, (g) general guidelines, and (h) writing the reflection.

Purpose

The main purpose of this type of project is to contribute to practice. This means that the purpose of the project is to come up with a solution or advice for the reader of the report, that is, the target audience. The purpose of the report is, therefore, to "convince the reader, as efficiently as possible, of the validity of your thesis" (Daniel 2013, p. 5).[1]

Target Audience

A distinction that was discussed in Chapter 4 was whether the project was based on a simulated situation, for example, anchored instruction, be oriented on a made-up or fictitious customer, or they can have a real customer. Each of these three alternative approaches has essentially two customers: the instructor and the client (whether real or fictitious). In most learning-oriented situations, the goal will be to practice writing the report for the client. This is, therefore, the target audience for the report. This means that, when writing, you have to keep this audience in mind.

---

[1] Note that, in some instances, the outcome of a project that contributes to practice does not involve a final report, but rather a product that is delivered, for instance, a database. The advice provided here is less relevant for those instances, but the deliverables to the client, as discussed in Chapter 7, remain important.

Although the instructor will read the report, the report should not be written for the instructor because the instructor is not the target audience. This means, for instance, that the report should not look like a class report or class assignment, but rather like a report written by consultants for a client.

The target audience influences, among other things, the information that is written in the report. For example, if the purpose of the report is to write a marketing plan for an existing company and the target audience is the CEO of the company, then there is no need to extensively explain the business this company is in because the CEO already knows this information!

Structure of the Report

The structure of the report is critical. When writing a report, it is recommended to start with developing the structure. Once the structure is clear, then writing becomes simply a matter of filling in the details. The structure for projects that contribute to practice are driven by the purpose. That is, the solution or opportunity. This leads to a different structure than the outcome of a project that contributes to theory. Typically, papers from a project that contributes to theory start with a question, provide a thorough background and literature review, describe the methods used, summarize the results of the analysis, and finally, present a conclusion. A report for a project that contributes to practice is very different. Like the research paper, a business report starts with a question (topic). But unlike the research paper, the business report quickly provides an answer (thesis). The answer is then supported by information that is factual, persuasive, and efficient (Daniel 2012). The key is that, essentially, your client asked you questions and now they want the answer. So, the answers are, therefore, the most important thing in your report. "You must organize your whole report around those answers and wave them in your readers' faces. State the answers in the beginning, elaborate on them one by one in the rest of the report; include only things that pertain to these answers; and be sure that the pertinence is always clear" (Daniel 2012, p. 4). In terms of organizing, "use subheadings not merely (1) to demarcate the segments but more importantly (2) to let the reader know what they're getting ready to read" (Daniel 2012, p. 5). The report starts with an executive summary and the table of contents. Then, it follows essentially the following structure:

Introduce: This is where you inform the reader what the rest of the report (or part thereof) will say and in what order.

Main: Here you follow the exact order as explained in the introduction. Use headings and subheadings so that the structure is clear and the reader knows what to expect for each part.

Conclusion: Here is where you summarize the main points.

References: This is where you provide information for the sources that you cited in the text.

Appendixes: Sometimes, it is useful to have appendixes. The appendixes are a place where you can explain something that falls outside of the main argument that goes from problem to solution.

This setup is followed for each part of your report so that essentially, the overall structure looks like this:

1. Executive summary
2. Table of contents
3. Introduction
4. Main
   a. A. Introduction
   b. A. Main
      i. a) Introduction
      ii. a) Main
         1. And, so on
      iii. a) Conclusion
      iv. b) And, so on
   c. A. Conclusion
   d. B. Introduction
   e. B. Main
   f. B. Conclusion
   g. And, so on

5. Conclusion

6. References

7. Appendixes

It is important that the executive summary and introduction to the report are not confused. To reiterate, in the introduction, you inform the reader what the rest of the report will say and in what order. The executive summary is a summary. It is similar to an abstract for an academic paper. It should be relatively short, and it should only summarize the most important parts of the report, such as the problem, the proposed solution, and some of the key data.

Throughout the report, you have to make decisions on what to include or leave out. This very much depends on the target audience. In some instances, it might be useful to include appendixes. For instance, the target audience may not be familiar with certain technical knowledge, but it may be distracting to explain all of this in the main text. In such a situation, it may be an option to include it in an appendix. For example, if you do an industry-level analysis and use the five-forces model (Porter 1980) and the target audience is not familiar with the five forces model, it may be an option to provide a technical discussion of the five-forces model in an appendix. That way, the main text can stay on track, for instance, focusing on the main results of the analysis, and leaving a more detailed description of what the five-forces model is and how it was applied for an appendix.

What goes in the main section of the report depends on the project purpose. Generally, the project report contains three types of information. First, a discussion and analysis of the problem, opportunity, or question. Second, a (theoretically) derived logical solution to that problem, or answer to the opportunity or research question. While a solution is nice, in itself, it is useless unless it can be implemented; therefore, a third topic that needs to be covered is a plan for implementation. The development of an implementation plan requires thinking that goes beyond the *theoretical situation*. What will be critical is to figure out the critical stakeholders. This means identifying who can help with the implementation and to get the critical people on board with any actions you recommend. It also means identifying who can stop the recommendations from being implemented (see for example, Barney and Gorman Clifford 2010, p. 6).

The Role of Theory, and Citing and Referencing

Solving problems, getting answers to questions or looking at ways to capitalize on opportunities requires research. "Research is one of the most misunderstood kinds of writing." (Daniel 2013, p. 119). For instance, research is *not* finding things and passing it along to others. Instead, a key task in research is to evaluate, for example, different sources, and to combine insights. Theories, for example, Ricardo's (1996) comparative advantage theory, and theoretical models, for example, Porter's (1990) Diamond model, play an important role in this process. These sources should be studied because they provide direction in the search process for solutions. For instance, a theory can provide insight into which variables are causally related or provide insight into what type of data should be collected.

Because the emphasis in projects that contribute to practice is on the solutions or answers, detailed descriptions and explanations of theories are often not meaningful or desired. Nevertheless, the sources that are consulted and used should always be documented so that your reader will know (1) how much faith to put in your findings, (2) where to go to check them out, and (3) where to go to read more about the subject (Daniel 2013, p. 139). A biography[2] is, therefore, *not* acceptable.

Formatting Guidelines

In terms of guidelines for writing reports, Daniels (2013, p. 3) states the following:

> When your boss tells you one thing and the book tells you something different, do what your boss says....Everything that has been said here, however, should be considered subject to being overruled by any special requirements you have been given for a particular assignment.

---

[2] A biography is summary list of sources that have been used in a project. This is not sufficient because it doesn't link specific statements or data or theories with a specific source. Therefore, it doesn't comply with the three reasons for providing documentations as stated by, for example, Daniel (2013).

This cannot be overstated and also goes back to the earlier statement about the importance of understanding the audience, and therefore knowing what kind of expectations the audience has. There are no single guidelines in terms of how to format a report. Different companies or people may expect different formatting, for example, in terms of font size, line separation, length of document, side margins, and so on. Some people may have expectations for the application of specific sets of rules, such as following APA style. APA stands for American Psychological Association, and while this style may be popular in some behavioral and social sciences, this does not mean it is the only desired or applied style. For example, in many business-related fields, referencing is preferred in Harvard style. The key, therefore, is that sources, such as Daniel (2013), can be used to give direction, but ultimately, what matters is what is expected by the target audience.

General Writing Guidelines

A project requires a meticulous approach toward finding sources, processing these sources, thinking about the content, keeping notes (See Daniel 2013, p. 129) and so on. Once a sufficient amount of data and material has been collected, the message for the target audience can be determined, that is, the solution or answer, and so on. It is important to continue data gathering until a point of *saturation* occurs. That is, where there is diminishing marginal contribution of additional data (Gummesson 1991). In other words, it is at this point in the data gathering process that previously gained insights continue to be confirmed and no new insights are gained. Only after reaching this point of saturation should you start writing the report. Starting to write before this point may mean that a lot of time is wasted as new insights can drastically change the message to the target audience and the content of the report. Starting to write too early can also lead to starting to think too far ahead and closing of options.

Once you start writing the report, it should be kept in mind that the report has to be understandable. Daniels (2013) identifies the five most common impediments to understandability, that is, the ease with which your point can be understood. These are:

- Failure to be neat
- Failure to write grammatically
- Failure to write appropriately and effectively
- Failure to organize
- Failure to make the organizational plan clear

A helpful strategy to avoid these failures is to start with the overall structure of the report as discussed earlier in this chapter. Using bulleted lists with the main points helps to think about the message for the target audience. It also helps with organizing this message, making sure the different parts are connected, and the logical flow of the argument, that is, how you will get your message across. Once this organization and logic are put down, it becomes a matter of filling in the details while keeping in mind conciseness, preciseness, forcefulness, and fluency (Daniel 2013, p. 26). Daniel (2013) also provides helpful advice on how to write good paragraphs following the classic four-part form Daniel (2013, p. 30):

1. Say it
2. Explain it
3. Detail it
4. Say it again

Graphs and tables should be used as much as possible in a report. For instance, "well-drawn graphs are tremendous attention grabbers and are more effective than many pages of prose in making the same point." (Daniel 2013, p. 100). For instance, a graph such as Figure 9.1 shows how the honey price to beekeepers and in retail stores has increased over time, while the gap between the two has been increasing. Key things to keep in mind are that graphs and tables should come after the discussion in the text, that they need to clearly show something and that they have appropriate labels.

Papers for Projects that Contribute to Theory

Similar to projects that contribute to practice, projects that contribute to theory can fall into different categories, such as task, discipline, or

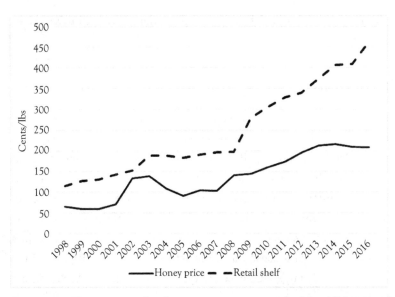

Figure 9.1 *Honey price development over time in the United States*

problem project; see Chapter 4. They can also be discovery- or utilization-oriented. As was explained in the section on projects that contribute to practice, these distinctions do not make a difference in terms of writing the paper.

There is extensive literature on how to write a research paper. For instance, sources such as Claudio (2016), Gastel and Day (2016), Glasman-Deal (2012), Gustavii (2008), and Lester and Lester (2015) can provide valuable insight into how to write about a project that contributes to theory. Sources such as Zikmund et al. (2012) can be useful as well and as they include information on different types of projects, the data gathering process, and they include advice on how to analyze data. Much of the information related to writing reports for projects that contribute to practice also apply to writing related to projects that contribute to theory, but a key difference is the purpose and the audience.

Purpose

The main purpose here is to contribute to theory. This means that the purpose is much more oriented on a theoretical discussion and coming up with new theoretical insights. The purpose, therefore, is clearly to communicate this new insight.

Target Audience

Similar to class projects that contribute to practice, class projects that contribute to theory have two potential target audiences: the instructor and academic community. Because in most learning-oriented situations the goal will be to practice writing the paper for the academic community, this is often the target audience for a paper. This target audience can be real, for example, a paper is submitted to a conference or academic journal,[3] or it can be fictitious, for example, a paper follows the guidelines for a conference or journal, but is not actually submitted. Papers written for an academic target audience are typically written *objectively* and use passive voice.

Structure of the Paper

The structure of academic papers generally contains the following parts; see also Chapter 6:

1. Abstract
2. Introduction
3. Literature review
4. Methodology
5. Data
6. Findings and discussion
7. Conclusion
8. References

---

[3] Please note that, in countries such as the United States, class projects can be conducted as part of the learning process, but if the goal is to publish the findings, and if it contains primary data collection, then typically approval by the university's Institutional Review Board (IRB) is required.

Some of this can vary depending on the exact purpose of project, that is, what it intends to contribute to theory, see Chapter 8, but a crucial part of projects that contribute to theory is that previous theory is shown (the literature review), and that based on the presented data, it is explained how new insight was gained, that is, a contribution to theory is made. A distinct difference in writing a report for a project that contributes to practice and a paper for a project that contributes to theory is that, in the former, due to the target audience, the solution is typically presented immediately, and following this, it is explained why or how that solution was developed, while in the latter, due to the target audience, the answer is only presented in the end. This is related to the objectivity and to let the target audience reach the same conclusions on its own. It is, therefore, critical to show why new insight is necessary, that is, what is wrong with what is currently known in the academic literature, and how the data and findings provide meaningful additional insight.

The Role of Theory, and Citing and Referencing

While theories and models are important for projects that contribute to practice in terms of application of models and because these provide direction for the project, that is, what data to collect, they are even more important in projects that contribute to theory. Furthermore, the emphasis in the report and paper is different. While in reports for projects that contribute to practice, the emphasis is on the practical side, and therefore, there is less emphasis on a discussion and explanation of the theories and models and more on the application of models, for a project that is contributing to theory, the theoretical discussion is critical. This discussion requires a carefully conducted analysis of the existing theories and insights into the substantive field of the study so that it can be explained to the target audience what is *wrong* with the literature, that is, where insight is missing or where current insights provide conflicting conclusions.

As with projects that contribute to practice, the same guidelines apply in terms of making sure that sources are appropriately identified. Thus, a bibliography is also not acceptable in papers for projects that contribute to theory.

Formatting Guidelines

The same guideline applies that was stated earlier "Everything that has been said here, however, should be considered subject to being overruled by any special requirements you have been given for a particular assignment… When your boss tells you one thing and the book tells you something different, do what your boss say (Daniel 2013, p. 3)," except in this case the boss is the journal or conference that is targeted. Academic outlets such as journals and conferences each have their own formatting guidelines. For instance, some academic outlets have very detailed formatting rules, *which* include font sizes. This is often the case for conferences that publish proceedings, but where the organization has limited editorial staff. They, therefore, need to make sure that all papers follow the same format, which often results in very detailed guidelines. Guidelines can vary considerably and relate to, for example, the length of a manuscript, the layout of a manuscript (for example, some outlets use two columns per page), and there are several different guidelines related to how the citing and referencing should occur and how they should be formatted. The key, therefore, is to familiarize yourself with the specific requirements that the target audience has.

General Guidelines

The general guidelines for writing papers as the result of a project that contributes to theory are similar to those that focus on contributing to practice. For example, it means following guidelines such as brevity, logic and clarity, and clean typing (Gustavii 2008). The goal is the same as for a report from a project that contributes to practice: get the message across as clear as possible and without distractions. While, for instance, verbose language may be useful and enjoyable when reading a novel, it has no place in business writing. This also means, for instance, that sentences such as "The highly esteemed and world renowned Michael Porter who has been a professor at the one of the best universities, that is, Harvard Business School, and who has been involved in many consulting projects and is widely seen as one of the primary contributors to strategic management, has developed the five-forces framework which…" are not acceptable. This should simply become "Porter's (1980) five forces framework…"

A difference in writing is when it occurs. While it is recommended that writing a report for a project that contributes to practice starts late, writing for a project that contributes to theory can start early. Some important reasons for this are that for a report on a project that contributes to practice, the solution is presented early in the report. Therefore, the solution should be known before the writing starts. The solution is only known toward the end of the project; therefore, the writing can only start toward the end of the project. The process for a project that contributes to theory, on the other hand, is directed by the literature review and the conclusions are only derived toward the end of the paper. Therefore, writing in this type of project can and should start earlier. In particular, the writing of the literature review will force thinking on the analysis of the literature and the logic of the argument related to the gap in the literature. This will aid the research process that is followed in the project.

Writing the Reflection

As was indicated in the discussion earlier, there are potentially two target audiences for both types of projects. While the purpose is usually to practice writing for the *real* target audience, another audience in the projects is the course instructor. Because the projects are part of an educational process, instructors typically have requirements that are focused on the learning and that may go beyond what would be communicated in a report to a client in a project that contributes to practice or a paper for an academic readership in a project that contributes to theory, and is therefore typically, a separate document. These requirements are often captured by asking students to reflect upon their experiences and learning from the project. Training this type of reflective thinking is considered a higher-order learning (level five in Bloom's taxonomy, see Chapter 2), and therefore has benefits that go beyond the specific project. Reflections can be written by a group or individually.

Similar guidelines apply as have been explained earlier. That means, in general, you have to think about the purpose of the reflection, the target audience, that is, the instructor, and whether there are specific formatting or other guidelines. The purpose of a written reflection is that students demonstrate their ability to reflect and learn, that is, thinking about and interpreting the project experience and determining what new understanding they have gained. Reflections usually deal with several topics such as learning about: (a) the topic area and (b) the process of doing the project such as what went well or could have gone better.

Presentations

In addition to writing a report or paper, the results of a project typically also have to be presented. For example, a presentation for the client, or at a conference, or simply in the classroom. There is extensive literature on how to present. For instance, sources such as Duarte (2008, 2010, 2012), Hoff (1992), and Karia (2015) can provide valuable insight into how to present. Many of the points made previously for writing also apply to presenting. This means that you need to understand the purpose of the presentation, and that you need to know who the target audience is. Some people make distinctions between different types of presentations such as: informative, instructional, arousing, persuasive, decision making, demonstrative, and inspirational. The following discussion is based on advice provided by Duarte (2008, 2010) because she provides valuable insight on how to deliver effective and engaging presentations that should impact the audience. Whether you present for a client or an academic audience, having an impact is a primary objective of a presentation. "Presentations have the power to change the world. The nexus of almost every movement and high-stakes decision relies on the spoken word to get traction, and presentations are a powerful platform to persuade" (Duarte 2010, p. 22).

Purpose of the Presentation

On the one hand, the purpose of the presentation is similar to that of the written document that accompanies the presentation. It presents the findings and conclusions that have been written in the project report or paper. Therefore, it presents the contribution that the project made to practice or theory. On the other hand, the purpose of the presentation is quite different from the written report or paper. If your presentation is simply presenting the exact same thing as the report with lots of text on your slides, then there is no need for the presentation because your target audience can simply read it.

All types of writing falls between the two extremes of reports and stories (Duarte 2010). Reports are documents that provide information and facts and emphasize accuracy, details, and so forth, and inform the target audience. Stories, on the other hand, are experiential and emotional and emphasize evocative and implied information. Stories entertain. Presentations fall in the middle and contain both information and stories. They emphasize explanation and to make meaning clear (Duarte 2010). The purpose of the presentation is most commonly to change the mind or behavior of the audience (Duarte 2010, p. 4).

Target Audience

In essence, the target audience for the presentation is similar to that for the report and paper, and if presented in class, the target audience can be other students unless the educational purpose is to practice presenting for the client or academic audience. So, in this regard, the determination of the target audience is the same as that for a project that contributes to practice or theory.

However, Duarte takes things a step further in terms of the audience. Duarte presents several key ideas that relate to the target audience and that have to be incorporated into the design of a presentation. First, a key idea brought forward by Duarte (2010) is that the effectiveness of a presentation depends on how well the message resonates with the audience. As a consequence, a main consideration is how to create this resonance. Second, and related to this is that this requires an understanding of the audience. To be able to create a resonating presentation requires knowing who the audience is and what resonates with them. This means asking questions such as: what are they like? Why are they there? What keeps them up at night? How can you solve their problem? What do you want them to do? How might they resist? How can you best reach them? (Duarte 2008, p. 15). Third, and related to the previous two points, Duarte (2010) suggests that the presentation can be viewed as taking the audience on a journey. Fourth, and related to all previous points, while in most presentations the presentation revolves around the presenter and reflects the agenda of the presenter, instead, it should be focused on the audience and build a connection with the audience (Duarte 2008, p. 4). This means that instead of the presenter being the hero in the journey, the audience is the hero in the journey and the presenter is more like a mentor (Duarte 2010, p. 20). While these may seem obvious, and while the difference in terms of who is the hero may seem subtle and many presenters claim that their presentation is for the audience, a presentation that is designed from scratch from the perspective of the audience is radically different and in our experience relatively rare in classroom situations.

Structure of the Presentation

With the aforementioned in mind, and with the goal of creating a presentation that resonates, a key question is then, how can such a presentation be designed and created? First, to create a good presentation takes time. Duarte estimates that she takes between 30 and 70 hours to create a presentation if the data has already been collected (Duarte 2008, p. 13). This would be the case if the presentation is designed after the report or paper has been written.

Second, a key idea behind the presentation is to create something visual and with limited text on slides.

> If a slide contains more than 75 words, it has become a document. You can either reduce the amount of content on the slide...or admit that this is a document and not a presentation...Presentations with 50 or so words per slide serve as a teleprompter. This less-than-engaging approach often results from a lack of time pent rehearsing the content, and is the default style of many professionals. Unfortunately, presenters who rely on the teleprompter approach also usually turn their backs to the audience. The audience may even perceive such presenters as slow, as the audience reads ahead and has to wait for the presenter to catch up...True presentations focus on the ...ideas and concepts they want to communicate. The slides reinforce the content visually rather than

create distraction…It takes an investment of time on the part of the presenter to develop and rehearse this type of content, but the results are worth it (Duarte 2008, p. 7).

To look at this differently, an audience will not read slides and listen to a presenter at the same time because reading and listening are conflicting activities. Visuals, on the other hand, can be used in combination with listening to somebody talk (Duarte 2008, p. 6).

Third, the overall structure of the presentation is the journey that the audience takes which alternates between facts and storytelling and which is organized around a big idea, the key message that you want to communicate in the presentation. This big idea must articulate your unique point of view, must convey what is at stake, and must be written in the form of a complete sentence, for example, "This software will make your team more productive and generate a million dollars in revenue over two years" (Duarte 2010, p. 78). Stories are used to create interest and can be specifically helpful to generate certain emotions. By telling stories, you are able to connect with an audience in an emotional way. The journey contains:

1. A beginning that contains a description of where the audience currently is. It does not have to be long and it ends with a call for adventure that relates to what could be.
2. A middle that contains contrasting content and that alternates between what is and what could be. Contrast in terms of content, emotion or delivery can be used to create resonance with the audience. The middle ends with a call to action that defines what the audience is expected to do.
3. An end that repeats the most important points. Similar to the beginning, it is shorter than the middle of the presentation, but it ends on a higher plane than the beginning.

Duarte (2010) uses the Sparkline as a tool to design presentations with the aforementioned in mind, see Figure 9.2 for an example. Note how the beginning and end are shorter than the middle, how the end is at a higher plane than the beginning, and how the middle is build up around contrast.

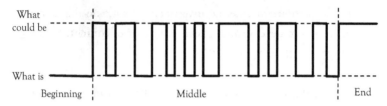

Figure 9.2 An example of a presentation Sparkline

The Role of Theory, and Citing and Referencing

The presentation is oriented on presenting some of the results of the project and is oriented around a big idea. This may have a component of theory in it, especially if the project is a project that contributes to theory. Depending on the importance of this theory, more or less attention may be given to it in the presentation.

As stated previously, the sources that are consulted and used should always be documented so that your reader will know (1) how much faith to put in your findings, (2) where to go to check them out, and (3) where to go to read more about the subject (Daniel 2013, p. 139). In the case of a presentation, there are two reasons why there is a limited need to provide citing and referencing information. First, the presentation slides have limited space, and it should be used as effectively as possible. Second, if the presentation is accompanied by a report or paper, then the citing and referencing information is already in the report or paper.

Formatting Guidelines

As was already explained, slides should have limited text. Font size is somewhat debatable but minimum font sizes for presentation slides are typically 24 or 28 pt. Data, for example, shown in graphs or tables are a an important part of presentations. In many instances, people present too much data on a single presentation slide. It is important to limit the cognitive complexity of slides and keeping it simple by, for example, focusing on a single message or point on each slide. While keeping in mind that the goal is to get the message across (while resonating with the audience), there should be as few distractions as possible. Therefore, things such as animations or logos on all slides are discouraged. It goes beyond the scope of this book to give detailed formatting guidelines for presentations, but Duarte (2008) provides extremely useful advice that is organized around key areas:

- How to arrange elements on an individual presentation slide. This deals with contrast, hierarchy, creating unity by dividing slides into columns, whitespace, proximity, and flow.
- How to use visual elements and dealing with items such as background, appropriate and meaningful color schemes, text, and the use of images.
- Movement on slides. While animations can easily become a distraction, there are situations in which having movement on the slides is useful.

General Presentation Guidelines

Presentations, and especially the type of presentations that have been discussed earlier, require experience. What should be kept in mind is that presentation skills get developed over time and that what is acceptable at one point in time may no longer be acceptable at another point in time. For example, when children learn to present, they typically find it challenging to present something, that is, stand in front of a group of people and talk. They may try to memorize an entire presentation, but may have to deal with learning to become comfortable with a lot of faces staring at them. Later, students may learn to use small note cards so that they can keep the presentation on track and they may learn to become more comfortable standing in front of a group of people. Students may also learn to use the presentation slides as prompts so that they don't have to memorize the entire presentation. As discussed, the idea presented here is to go beyond these issues and create dynamic and effective presentations that resonate with an audience and that ideally will be remembered for a long time because that would mean that it had an impact.[4]

---

[4] Sometimes, people misunderstand the difference between an audience that is engaged or involved and a presentation that resonates with an audience. For example, one idea used in presentations is to reward the audience for sticking

Conclusion

This chapter covered the aspect of communicating the results of the project to the target audience. Two forms of communication were discussed: a written report or paper and an oral presentation. It was noted that, for some projects that contribute to practice, the project outcome may not entail a written document because it may instead be another type of product such as a software application. For both written and oral communication, the most important aspect is to understand the audience. This relates to formatting aspects as well as the content of the message and means that the author or presenter has to carefully consider the needs of the audience. Differences between project reports from projects that contribute to practice versus papers from projects that contribute to theory were discussed. Presentations are different from written works and should be based on visual elements. Key considerations are to create a resonating presentations by designing a Sparkline around a journey in which the audience is the hero and by using storytelling.

---

with it by, for example, asking questions and providing a treat such as candy for those who answer. The audience member who provides the answer is then considered engaged with the presentation. This is quite different from a presentation that resonates with an audience. In a resonating presentation, there is no reason to provide the audience with bribes such as candy because a resonating audience in a way can't wait to hear what the presenter will say next. For a resonating presentation, the message of the presentation will be remembered. For a presentation where the audience is encouraged to pay attention by bribing them with candy, at best, the handing out of candy might be remembered.

CHAPTER 10

Conclusion

The current generation of graduates from U.S. universities faces challenges with finding appropriate employment. Connected to this, it has been shown that students have limited improvements in skills such as critical thinking while attending universities. Part of the reason for this lack of improvement might be caused by the traditional method of education in the United States. This is the lecture style format that has been shown to have severe disadvantages in terms of the match with higher-level learning skills. Active learning approaches provide advantages for students and are a better match in terms of higher-level learning skills. One such approach is project-based learning, which was the topic of this book. The information in this book is based on a mix of knowledge gained from academic studies as well as personal experience. The purpose of this book was to provide students with a background on project-based learning as well as practical advice on how to approach projects in classroom situations.

The first chapters in the book were mostly theory-oriented. Some of this information went beyond what students normally experience in classrooms, for example, a topic such as Bloom's taxonomy. It was, nevertheless, deemed necessary to delve into these aspects to explain why project-based learning is an appealing alternative to more traditional approaches and what students can learn by following this type of approach. Especially in active learning approaches where students have a deeper involvement in their own learning, it is necessary for students to gain insight into the teaching and learning processes such as those followed in project-based learning approaches. As Chapter 4 showed, and critical for students to understand, there is not one approach to projects. While a lecture format is a standard format with little deviation, the project-based approach has many different dimensions. A clear classification scheme for project-based learning does not yet exist, and in this book, therefore, some of the important dimensions were discussed. This included delineating projects that contribute to practice from those that contribute to theory, separating projects that are discovery-oriented where students use the project context to find and learn about relevant theories versus projects that are utilization-oriented where students already mostly possess the relevant knowledge and apply it in practical situations, and distinguishing projects with more or less instructor guidance (task, discipline, and problem) and an environment with more or less uncertainty (simple, complicated, complex, or chaos).

With the fundamentals in place, the book moved to the more practical side of things by delving into four issues. First, the aspects of teams was discussed. Two major takeaways from this discussion should be that collections of individuals don't automatically make a team, and conflict is a necessary part of team building. Many classroom projects with teams encounter problems, and in many of these instances, trying to avoid conflict and not communicating are key concerns that prohibit a collection of individuals to become a high-performing student team. Advice was provided to increase the likelihood of a successful team, such as utilizing team contracts and peer evaluations. Separate chapters were devoted to projects that contribute to practice and projects that contribute to theory. Due to the different clients involved, projects that contribute to practice can be quite varied. The discussion, therefore, centered around the five basic processes that occur in projects (initiate, plan, execute, monitor and control, and closing), and advice was provided on how to deal with these processes in particular related to client communication. Projects that contribute to theory lead to more standardized outcomes and the discussion, therefore, focused on the different parts of the final paper. For example, advice was provided on how to approach a literature review and methodology section. For the projects that contribute to practice as well as the projects that contribute to theory, it is imperative for students to know and have a deep understanding of theories. Without this, it is, for instance, not possible to do the correct application of a business tool. Lastly, there was a discussion on communicating the results.

It is our hope that this book provides helpful practical guidance for students so that their learning from and through project-based learning improves. From an educator's perspective, the ultimate goal is to improve student learning. While learning-oriented approaches place more responsibility for learning with the students, instructors can help by providing guidance and direction. In particular, the appendixes provide many tools and examples that were included to make it a practically useful book.

APPENDIX A

Examples of Team Agreements

Example 1: Team Contract for Developing an Export Plan for a U.S. Company to Japan

Group members:

- Jennifer
- Kazuki
- Nikita
- Henk

Type of project: Consultancy
Target audience: Client/Owner of a soap company
Product: Soap

Group members' responsibilities:

Phase 1 written portion: Kazuki
Phase 1 presentation: Jennifer
Phase 2 written portion: Nikita
Phase 2 presentation: Nikita
Phase 3 written portion: Jennifer
Phase 3 presentation: Henk
Phase 4 written portion: Henk
Phase 4 presentation: Kazuki

Phase 1: Initial macro environment analysis
- Analyze host country: United States
- Analyze target country: Japan

- Assess risks
  - Cross cultural: Kazuki
  - Country: Jennifer
  - Commercial: Henk
  - Currency: Nikita
- Conduct macro environment analysis
  - Japan's economic analysis: Nikita
    - Compared to United States
  - Japan's legal analysis: Jennifer
    - Compared to United States
  - Japan's political analysis: Jennifer
    - Compared to United States
  - Japan's environmental analysis: Henk
    - Compared to United States
  - Japan's technological analysis: Henk
    - Compared to United States
  - Japan's social analysis: Kazuki
    - Compared to United States
  - Type basic bullet points of information: Jennifer
  - Work on the Part 1 written portion: Kazuki
  - Edit paper: Henk
  - Print paper: Nikita
  - Create slides for PowerPoint: Jennifer
  - Edit PowerPoint slides: Nikita

Phase 2: Improve Phase 1 and add initial industry-level analysis

- Each group member is responsible for staying up to date on information related to Phase 1
- Industry analysis
  - Size and growth rate: Nikita
  - Trade barriers: Jennifer
  - Standards and regulations: Henk
  - Customer preferences: Kazuki

- Competitor analysis: Jennifer and Kazuki
  - Competitors will be identified and then split between two people
  - Research possible competitors and their success in the foreign market
  - Look for advantages that competitors might have
- Value proposition: Nikita

Phase 3: Improve Phases 1 and 2 and add your path forward

- Entry mode analysis: Nikita
- Partner analysis: Kazuki
- Implementation plan: Jennifer

Phase 4: Improve all phases and add detail for the implementation plan

- Human resources: Henk
- Marketing: Jennifer
- Finance: Nikita

Group expectations

- Equal participation
- Must provide more information if asked by a fellow group member
- Response time of no more than a day (response can be "I'll get back to you on that")
- Notes must be provided with all research
- Notes must be on the group's Google Docs for easy access for all group members

Peer evaluation form	Very good	Good	Okay	Bad	Very bad
The group member was prepared for group meetings	5	4	3	2	1
Work was completed in a timely manner	5	4	3	2	1
The group member contributed to an in-depth research	5	4	3	2	1
The group member was understanding cultural differences	5	4	3	2	1
The group member had a good attitude	5	4	3	2	1

Group meetings
Every Tuesday at 5:00 pm in Learning Commons

We agree to:

- Come to class.
- Make sure that, if we miss a class, we contact others in our group.
- That we will work on group assignments collaboratively.
- Show up for the meetings.
- Make sure that, if we miss a meeting, we contact others in our group.
- Complete research or assignments before group meetings, so that discussion is the main focus.
- Assist others having trouble with the assignments.

This group contract is binding upon all who sign it and is subject to change with prior approval of all members of the group.

Signature: Jennifer _____   Date:_____
Signature: Kazuki _____   Date:_____
Signature: Nikita _____   Date:_____
Signature: Henk _____   Date:_____

Example 2: General Setup for a Team Contract

Team Contract

Group Members

Name	E-mail	Phone
Daniela		
Svetlana		
Sverre		
Lee		

Team Communication

Primary: Face-to-face meetings

Secondary: E-mail, text messaging, phone call

Functional Roles

Co-leaders: Daniela, Svetlana, Sverre, and Lee

All need to report to each other for any information. All need to exhibit openness, equality, empathy, be supportive, and positive.

Process Roles

Leader: Daniela—Contacts other partners and sends reminders of meetings

Facilitator and scribe: Svetlana and Sverre—Document *everything*

Editor or Checker: Lee

Submitter: Daniela

Roles subject to change each week.

Peer Evaluation Form for Group Work

Your name _____

Write the name of each of your group members in a separate column. For each person, indicate the extent to which you agree with the statement on the left, using a scale of 1–4 (1 = strongly disagree; 2 = disagree; 3 = agree; 4 = strongly agree). Total the numbers in each column.

Evaluation criteria	Group member:	Group member:	Group member:	Group member:
Attends group meetings regularly and arrives on time.				
Contributes meaningfully to group discussions.				
Completes group assignments on time.				
Prepares work in a quality manner.				
Demonstrates a cooperative and supportive attitude.				
Contributes significantly to the success of the project.				
Totals				

Feedback on Team Dynamics

1. How effectively did your group work?
2. Were the behaviors of any of your team members particularly valuable or detrimental to the team? Explain.
3. What did you learn about working in a group from this project that you will carry into your next group experience?

Team Expectations

- Show up for group meetings on time
- Complete delegated work by the end of the day (when discussed)
- Participate equally with ideas, workload, notes, speaking, or writing
- Come to class to discuss things with teammates
- Conduct research and produce quality work
- Act professionally and responsibly
- Effectively communicate qualitative and quantitative information in speaking, writing, and presenting

Print: _____

Signature: _____ Date: _____

Print: _____

Signature: _____ Date: _____

Print: _____

Signature: _____ Date: _____

Print: _____

Signature: _____ Date: _____

Example 3: Initial Team Contract for Developing an Export Plan for a U.S. Company to Japan

Individual Responsibilities for Phase One of the Project

Group member	Responsibilities
Kjeld	Conduct research; allocated research area and topic (we will share the bulk), will write about the designated, specific findings that are related to the model that we will follow that had been introduced in the class.
Shani	Conduct research; allocated research area and topic (we will share the bulk), will write about the designated, specific findings that are related to the model that we will follow that had been introduced in the class.
Olga	Conduct research; allocated research area and topic (we will share the bulk), will write about the designated, specific findings that are related to the model that we will follow that had been introduced in the class.
Miho	Conduct research; allocated research area and topic (we will share the bulk), will write about the designated, specific findings that are related to the model that we will follow that had been introduced in the class.

Performance Criteria

Each person would receive an individual judgment regarding these criteria.

Criteria	NO	1	2	3	4
Teamwork (Does the team member work well with others and show the necessary respect to achieve the objectives?)					
Contribution and participation (Does the team member show up for meetings prepared to discuss the topics needed to complete the tasks? Does the team member ask pointed and relevant questions about the topics?)					
Supporting material (Is the research material relevant and useful?)					
Composition (Is the final product readable and useful toward the end goal of presenting a proposal to the company to determine whether expanding their product to Australia is viable?)					

Contract

- The group will meet twice a week in order to keep up to date on the steps toward each deadline that must be met in order to produce a successful project.
- Participation in the group is a must in order to be fair to one another.
- Contribution to the overall team effort.
- Willingness to participate and research, with a ready-to-learn attitude.
- Consideration of others within the group, along with common courtesy in regards to whatever may come up that might affect the team.
- Carry out the practice of being punctual and meet the proposed deadlines.
- Complete all research duties on time prior to meeting to discuss.

Example 4: Team-Developed Peer Evaluation Based on Points

Points possible: 60 points

10 points: Attends group meetings regularly and arrives on time.

10 points: Contributes to group discussions.

10 points: Completes group assignments on time.

10 points: Prepares work in a quality manner.

10 points: Demonstrates a cooperative and supportive attitude.

10 points: Contributes to the success of the project.

APPENDIX B

Example Form Student Waiver

Student Off-Campus Acknowledgment and Assumption of Risk, Release from Liability, and Hold Harmless Agreement

_____

Student identification number

I, _____, am a student at [name of the university].
    (Student's full name)

I have voluntarily elected, instead of taking advantage of in-class resources and time, to pursue certain off-campus activities (the *activities*) to gather academic or educational information that I intend to incorporate into my coursework at the university in the following course: Course Number/Name/Professor:

_____.

I recognize that the activities are not a requirement of the course, nor any other coursework at the university. I voluntarily choose to pursue the activity and acknowledge and agree that I could satisfy the course requirements without engaging in the activities. The activities will include the following: [insert brief description, location, amount of time expected and identify any dangerous elements]

_____

_____

I am aware of the dangers involved in traveling off campus and engaging in the activities, and I am aware that there are special concerns and additional dangers associated with the following: [identify any unique risk factors, transportation risks, dangerous or unsupervised location, and other unknown elements]

_____

_____

I am aware of all of the risks aforementioned, and I am willing to assume those risks by participating in the activities, including but not limited to the risk that the activities may result in loss of personal property, bodily injury, or even death.

I also promise to conduct myself in a way that will not bring discredit to [name of university] and will not create an increased risk of harm to myself or others from [name of university].

I hereby voluntarily assume all such risks associated with the activities by signing underneath and participating in the activities and disclaim any claims, rights, or other legal claims that I may have against the university related in any way to my pursuit of the activities. I hereby covenant that I will not commence, prosecute, cause, or permit to be prosecuted, any action at law or in equity, nor any proceeding whatsoever, related in any way to my participation in the activities, whether for property damage or personal injury, in any court, arbitration, administrative, or other proceeding against the university, its affiliates and any trustees, officers, directors, faculty, staff, employees, volunteers, and agents. I agree to save, indemnify, defend, and hold harmless, [name of university], its affiliates, and any trustees, officers, directors, faculty, staff, employees, volunteers, and agents from any and all liability, claims, causes of action, or demands of any kind and nature whatsoever, including without limitation loss of personal property, personal injury, or death, which may arise from or in connection with the activities, and also including attorneys' fees and damages associated with defense of any claims.

The terms hereof shall serve as an acknowledgment and assumption of risk, release from liability, and hold harmless agreement, for me, my parents or guardians, my heirs, estate, executor, administrator, assignees, and all members of my family. I have read and understand this acknowledgment and assumption of risk, release from liability, and hold harmless agreement, and execute it as a free and voluntary act. Further, this acknowledgment and assumption of risk, release from liability and hold harmless agreement is contractual and not a mere recital.

I hereby represent and warrant that I am over the age of 18 years old.

---   ------------------

Signature of the student   Date

Or: I am under the age of 18 and have included the signature of a parent or legal guardian.

---   ------------------

Signature of the parent or legal guardian of student   Date
(If the student is younger than 18 years of age)

APPENDIX C

Examples of Nondisclosure Agreements

Example 1: Short Confidentiality Agreement

Group project at [name of the university] for [course] during [academic term]

I understand that all materials for the group project in this course are confidential and belong to the professor and the client. I may not, at any time, share this information with competing entities of my client, including direct and indirect competitors now or within the next five years. I further agree not to pass any information about my client or the project through any social media or Internet programs, including but not all-inclusive are: Dropbox, Facebook, Google Docs, Instagram, LinkedIn, My Space, and Twitter. I agree to use the Blackboard LMS (learning management system) to share any course information and materials for this course.

_____

Print the full name clearly

_____

Signature

_____

Date

Example 2: Example of a Medium Length Nondisclosure Agreement

This Confidentiality Agreement (*Agreement*) is made and effective the first day of the semester, [date]. This agreement governs all ideas, concepts, and business plans shared during the class and during class preparation between the client, instructor, guest speakers, and students. The Owner is defined as the person who shared the ideas, concepts, and/or business plan. The Recipient is defined as any registered student in [course], instructor, and/or guest speaker.

1. Confidential Information

The Owner proposes to disclose certain of its confidential and proprietary information (the *confidential information*) to the Recipient. Confidential information shall include all data, materials, products, technology, computer programs, specifications, manuals, business plans, software, marketing plans, business plans, financial information, and other information disclosed or submitted, orally, in writing, or by any other media, to the Recipient by the Owner. Nothing herein shall require the Owner to disclose any of its information.

2. Recipient's Obligations

The Recipient agrees that the confidential information is to be considered confidential and proprietary to the Owner, and the Recipient shall hold the same in confidence, shall not use the confidential information other than for the purposes of its business with the Owner. The Recipient will not disclose, publish, or otherwise reveal any of the confidential information received from the Owner to any other party whatsoever, except with the specific prior written authorization of the Owner.

3. Confidential information

Confidential information furnished in tangible form shall not be duplicated by the Recipient, except for purposes of this agreement. Upon the request of the Owner, the Recipient shall return all the confidential information received in written or tangible form, including copies, or reproductions or other media containing such confidential information, within ten (10) days of such request. At Recipient's option, any documents or other media developed by the Recipient containing the confidential information may be destroyed by the Recipient. The Recipient shall provide a written certificate to the Owner regarding destruction within ten (10) days thereafter.

4. No Implied Waiver

Either party's failure to insist in any one or more instances upon strict performance by the other party of any of the terms of this agreement shall not be construed as a waiver of any continuing or subsequent failure to perform or delay in performance of any term hereof.

By signing the agreement, I agree to hold all information, ideas, concepts, or business plans as confidential.

_____

Signature   *Printed* name   Date

Example 3: Example of a Detailed Nondisclosure Agreement

Mutual Nondisclosure Agreement

This Mutual Nondisclosure Agreement (this *Agreement*), effective [date] (*Effective Date*), is entered into by and between; [company, location and representatives] *and*;

Name of the receiving party: _____;

Address: _____;

Phone and E-mail: _____;

; (each herein referred to individually as a *Party*, or collectively as the *Parties*). In consideration of the covenants and conditions contained herein, the Parties hereby agree to the following:

1. Purpose

The Parties wish to explore discussions and business model, economic and marketing development related to [company or company product] of mutual interest (the *Opportunity*), and in connection with the disclosure of special uses, each Party has disclosed, and may further disclose certain confidential technical and business information (in such capacity, a Party disclosing the information, the *Discloser*) to the other Party (in such capacity, a Party receiving the information, the *Recipient*), that the Discloser desires the Recipient to treat as confidential.

2. Confidential Information

(a) *Definition. Confidential information* means: (i) any information (including any and all combinations of individual items of information) disclosed (directly or indirectly) by the Discloser to the Recipient pursuant to this agreement that is in written, graphic, machine-readable, or other tangible form (including, without limitation, financial disclosures, real estate, real-estate appraisals, purchases, leases, real-estate joint ventures, annual revenues, budgets, research, product plans, products, services, equipment, customers, markets, software, algorithms, inventions, discoveries, ideas, processes, designs, drawings, formulations, specifications, product con-figuration information, marketing and finance documents, prototypes, samples, datasets, and equipment) and is marked *Confidential, Propri-etary*, or in some other manner to indicate its confidential nature and (ii) oral information disclosed (directly or indirectly) by the Discloser to the Recipient pursuant to this agreement, provided that such information is designated as confidential at the time of its initial disclosure and reduced to a written summary by Discloser that is marked in a manner to indicate its confidential nature and delivered to the Recipient within thirty (30) days after its initial disclosure. Confidential information may include information of a third party that is in the possession of the Discloser and is disclosed to the Recipient under this agreement.

Exceptions. Confidential information shall not, however, include any information that: (i) was publicly known or made generally available with-out a duty of confidentiality prior to the time of disclosure by the Discloser to the Recipient; (ii) becomes publicly known or made generally available without a duty of confidentiality after disclosure by the Discloser to the Recipient through no wrongful action or inaction of the Recipient; (iii) is in the rightful possession of the Recipient without confidentiality obliga-tions at the time of disclosure by the Discloser to the Recipient as shown by the Recipient's then-contemporaneous written files and records kept in the ordinary course of business; (iv) is obtained by the Recipient from a third party without an accompanying duty of confidentiality and without a breach of such third-party's obligations of confidentiality; or (v) is inde-pendently developed by the Recipient without use of or reference to the Discloser's confidential information, as shown by written records and other competent evidence prepared contemporaneously with such independent development, provided that any combination of individual items of infor-mation shall not be deemed to be within any of the foregoing exceptions merely because one or more of the individual items are within such excep-tion, unless the combination as a whole is within such exception.

(b) *Compelled Disclosure.* If the Recipient becomes legally compelled to disclose any confidential information, other than pursuant to a con-fidentiality agreement, the Recipient will provide the Discloser prompt written notice, if legally permissible, and will use its best efforts to assist the Discloser in seeking a protective order or another appropriate remedy.

If the Discloser waives the Recipient's compliance with this agreement or fails to obtain a protective order or other appropriate remedy, the Recipient will furnish only that portion of the confidential information that is legally required to be disclosed, provided that any confidential information so disclosed shall maintain its confidentiality protection for all purposes other than such legally compelled disclosure.

3. Nonuse and Nondisclosure

The Recipient shall not use any confidential information of the Discloser for any purpose except to evaluate and engage in discussions concerning the opportunity. The Recipient shall not disclose any confidential information of the Discloser to third parties or to the Recipient's employees, except that, subject to the following Section 4, the Recipient may disclose the Discloser's confidential information to those employees of the Recipient who are required to have such information in order to evaluate or engage in discussions concerning the opportunity. The Recipient shall not reverse-engineer, disassemble, or decompile any prototypes, software, samples, or other tangible objects that embody the Discloser's confidential information and that are provided to the Recipient under this agreement.

4. Maintenance of Confidentiality

The Recipient shall take reasonable measures to protect the secrecy of and avoid disclosure and unauthorized use of the confidential information of the Discloser. Without limiting the foregoing, the Recipient shall take at least those measures that it employs to protect its own confidential information of a similar nature and shall ensure that its employees who have access to confidential information of the Discloser have signed a nonuse and nondisclosure agreement in content at least as protective of the Discloser and its confidential information as the provisions of this agreement, prior to any disclosure of the Discloser's confidential information to such employees. The Recipient shall reproduce the Discloser's proprietary rights notices on any such authorized copies in the same manner in which such notices were set forth in or on the original. The Recipient shall promptly notify the Discloser of any unauthorized use or disclosure, or suspected unauthorized use or disclosure, of the Discloser's confidential information of which the Recipient becomes aware.

5. No Obligation

Nothing in this agreement shall obligate either Party to proceed with any transaction between them, and each Party reserves the right, in its sole discretion, to terminate the discussions contemplated by this agreement concerning the opportunity. Nothing in this agreement shall be construed to restrict either Party's use or disclosure of its own confidential information.

6. No Warranty

All confidential information is provided "as is." Neither party makes any warranties, express, implied or otherwise, regarding the accuracy, completeness, or performance of any confidential information, or with respect to noninfringement or other violation of any intellectual property rights of a third party or of the Recipient.

7. Return of Materials

All documents and other tangible objects containing or representing the confidential information that has been disclosed by the Discloser to the Recipient, and all copies or extracts thereof or notes derived from there that are in the possession of the Recipient, shall be and remain the property of the Discloser and shall be promptly returned to the Discloser or destroyed (with proof of such destruction), each upon Discloser's written request.

8. No License

Nothing in this agreement is intended to grant any rights to the Recipient under any patent, mask work right, or copyright of the Discloser, nor shall this agreement grant the Recipient any rights in or to the confidential information of the Discloser, except as expressly set forth in this agreement.

9. Export Restrictions

Any software and other technical information disclosed under this agreement may be subject to restrictions and controls imposed by the Export Administration Act, Export Administration Regulations, and other laws and regulations of the United States and any other applicable government or jurisdiction, as enacted from time to time (the *Acts*). The Parties shall comply with all restrictions and controls imposed by the Acts.

10. Term

This agreement will remain in effect for a period of two (2) years after the effective date; provided that the obligations of the Recipient under this agreement shall survive, with respect to each particular item of confidential information of the Discloser, until five (5) years after disclosure thereof to the Recipient hereunder.

11. Remedies

The Recipient agrees that any violation or threatened violation of this agreement may cause irreparable injury to the Discloser, entitling the Discloser to seek injunctive relief in addition to all legal remedies.

12. Miscellaneous

This agreement shall bind and inure to the benefit of the Parties and their respective successors and permitted assigns. Neither Party may assign or otherwise transfer this agreement without the prior written consent of the other Party, except that either Party may assign this agreement without consent in connection with a merger, reorganization, consolidation, change of control, or sale of all or substantially all of the assets to which this agreement pertains, provided that the assigning Party provides a prompt written notice to the other Party of any such permitted assignment. Any assignment or transfer of this agreement in violation of the foregoing shall be null and void. This agreement will be interpreted and construed in accordance with the laws of the [state], without regard to conflict of law principles. Each Party hereby represents and warrants that the persons executing this agreement on its behalf have express authority to do so, and in so doing, to bind such Party thereto. This agreement contains the entire agreement between the Parties with respect to the opportunity and supersedes all prior written and oral agreements between the Parties regarding the opportunity. The Recipient shall not have any obligation, express or implied by law, with respect to trade secret or proprietary information of the Discloser disclosed under this agreement, except as set forth herein.

If a court or other body of competent jurisdiction finds any provision of this agreement, or portion thereof, to be invalid or unenforceable, such provision will be enforced to the maximum extent permissible so as to effect the intent of the Parties, and the remainder of this agreement will continue in full force and effect. No provision of this agreement may be waived except by a writing executed by the Party against whom the waiver is to be effective. A Party's failure to enforce any provision of this agreement shall neither be construed as a waiver of the provision nor prevent the Party from enforcing any other provision of this agreement. No provision of this agreement may be amended or otherwise modified except by a writing signed by the Parties to this agreement. The Parties may execute this agreement in counterparts, each of which shall be deemed as original, but all of which together constitute one and the same agreement. This agreement may be delivered by facsimile transmission, and facsimile copies of executed signature pages shall be binding as originals.

13. Disputes

All disputes arising out of this agreement will be subject to the exclusive jurisdiction and venue of the state courts located in [state], and each Party hereby consents to the personal jurisdiction thereof.

In witness whereof, the Parties by their duly authorized representatives have executed this agreement as of the effective date.

[Company]
By: [Signature]

Name: [Company representative] Print name: _____
Title: Authorized signatory
Dated: [date]_____, [year]

Receiving Party
By: [Signature]

Print name [student, instructor, administrator name] _____
Dated: [date] _____, [year]

APPENDIX D

Example of Team Charter

Background

Client Strategy

With today's technology and information literally at the tips of our fingers, we need to educate ourselves, so we can keep our children as safe as possible while utilizing the tools and features that cell phones have to offer. All it takes is one wrong word in a search engine or one wrong push of the screen and a child can end up with information to which they should not be privy.

Business Case

As technology becomes increasingly present in children's lives, the more likely they can be exposed to and at risk of inappropriate content online. From a social need perspective, the successful training of parents can result in the increased safety for children while using smart devices, such as an iPhone.

Project Description

High-Level Objectives

The goal is to *protect children* by keeping them safe from Internet exploitation such as online bullying, *child* pornography, *child* abuse, and blackmail as a result of Internet exploitation or social media (including chat rooms, text messaging, photos, electronic mail, and peer-to-peer software).

The purpose is to *educate parents* so that they can be equipped with the requisite knowledge, skills, and abilities to counter any Internet exploitation of children and protect their own family.

Project Outputs and Activities

Outputs and associated activities (the work breakdown structure, WBS) are listed as follows:

Output 1.0: Published Curriculum.

1.1 Determine training modules.

1.2 Research application technologies.

1.3 Research project legalities.

1.4 Develop training curriculum.

1.5 Test training modules.

1.6 Validate curriculum.

1.7 Publish curriculum.

Output 2.0: Trained Parents.

2.1 Conduct cell phone dangers training.

2.2 Conduct cell phone protection training.

2.3 Conduct parental involvement training.

Output 3.0: Project Management.

3.1 Form a project team.

3.2 Propose and select a project.

3.3 Develop a project charter.

3.4 Develop a project plan.

3.5 Provide status reports (x2).

3.6 Evaluate a project.

Risks

As with any project, there will be some risks involved that may not be avoidable, but we must do our best to mitigate them.

High-Level Risks

The training will only help to make children safer online if the parents enforce the parental tools they have learned every day after the training. Due to the constantly changing technological landscape, newer threats come into existence every day. There may be new threats faced by parents, which are not covered in the course.

Implementation Risks

The internal risk factors include not being able to cover every single iPhone safety feature available and not being able to identify every single threat out there against children. In providing this training, there is an assumption that the parents or guardians will not only learn the tools available to them to help their children be safer on the Web, but that they will actually employ the methods that are covered in the instructor-led training. Another limit would be the ability for all parents to have access to the course due to time constraints or busy work or home schedules.

Team

Team members and their roles are listed in Table D.1.

Table D.1 Team roles

Team member	Role
1. Jin Asato	Trainer
2. Syd Green	Developer
3. Kim Leung	Developer or Project manager
4. Jan Smith	Software engineer

Schedule

Estimated completion dates for the outputs and associated activities are listed in Table D.2.

Table D.2 Summary schedule

Project outputs	Estimated completion date
1. Published curriculum	October 01
2. Trained parents	November 01
3. Project management	December 01

Key Stakeholders

The key stakeholders in this project are parents, children, and training developers. Parents and the training developers will be the key players in this project because the success of this project is dependent on an insightful and educational program that is easy to understand and meets the needs of the parents. The software application developers' stake in this project will be to create applications that meet the requirements of the training developers. Trainers will implement the training. See a summary of stakeholders, their interests, and their priority to the project in Table D.3.

Table D.3 Stakeholder analysis

Stakeholder	Interests	Priority
Parents	Protecting children	High
Children	Safe online presence	High
Training developers	Develop quality training material	High
Trainer	Train with quality material	Medium
Software application developers	Creating apps that can be safely monitored by parents	Medium

Team sign-off:

_____

_____

_____

_____

Example of a Project Management Plan

Project Management Plan

Background

With today's technology and information literally at the tips of our fingers, we need to educate ourselves, so we can keep our children as safe as possible while utilizing the tools and features that cell phones have to offer. All it takes is one wrong word in a search engine or one wrong push of the screen and a child can end up with information they should not be privy to.

Problem

As technology becomes increasingly present in children's lives, the more likely they can be exposed to and at risk of inappropriate content online. Catching a child in the wrong place or doing something inappropriate has caused a work–family conflict.

Solution

It has been discovered that there are several areas that parents need to educate themselves in. The features covered will be centered on Apple's iPhone. The online resources will be able to be utilized, no matter which phone. We will discuss involvement, parental controls, applications (apps), bullying, and resources in order to keep your child safe. Implement the controls, use the resources, have a contract, and maintain trust with your child. You should sleep easier knowing you have done what you can to keep them safe.

Beneficiaries

The key stakeholders in this project are parents and children. Parents and children will be the key players in this project because the success of this project is dependent on the actions of both parties. The parents must use what they learn, and the children must respond in such a way that would make their online presence safer.

Training developers and trainers will play a key role as well. Their purpose is to develop and implement an insightful and educational program that is easy to understand and meets the needs of the parents.

Method

The main two methods we are utilizing to keep develop our training program are project lifecycle and managing by objectives (MBO). The basic characteristics are being utilized according to the PMBOK for our project lifecycle approach. We have started our project by creating the project charter. From there, we are collecting information and organizing it to put into our presentations (organizing and preparing). Once the course is designed, we will test it, make corrections, and deliver the final product to our target audience (carrying out the project work). Upon completion, we can close our project.

Objectives

Goal

The goal is to *protect children* by keeping them safe from Internet exploitation such as online bullying, *child* pornography, *child* abuse, and blackmail as a result of Internet exploitation or social media (including chat rooms, text messaging, photos, electronic mail, and peer-to-peer software).

Purpose

The purpose is to *educate parents* so that they can be equipped with the requisite knowledge, skills, and abilities to counter any Internet exploitation of children and protect their own family. To do so effectively will require several presentations involving a tutorial of the application (30 minutes) and three hands-on application sessions (30 minutes each).

Outputs

The outputs (the deliverables) defining the project are as follows:

1. Published curriculum. 100 percent final training product by the end of course
2. Trained parents. 90 percent of parents trained by October 2018.
3. Project management. PM deliverables by the end of course.

Work Breakdown Structure

1. Published curriculum:
   1.1 Determine training modules.
   1.2 Research application technologies.
   1.3 Research project legalities.
   1.4 Develop training curriculum.
   1.5 Test training modules.
   1.6 Validate curriculum.
   1.7 Publish curriculum.
2. Trained Parents:
   2.1 Conduct cell phone dangers training.
   2.2 Conduct cell phone protection training.
   2.3 Conduct parental involvement training.
3. Project Management:
   3.1 Form a project team.
   3.2 Propose and select a project.
   3.3 Develop a project charter.
   3.4 Develop a project plan.
   3.5 Provide status report 1.
   3.6 Provide status report 2.
   3.7 Evaluate the project.
   3.8 Report and record results.

Work Breakdown Structure Dictionary

1. *Published curriculum:*
   1.1 Determine training modules. Determine what material to cover in training. Survey most common child cell phone safety issues.
   1.2 Research application technologies. Look at what applications are frequently used by children on an iPhone.
   1.3 Research project legalities. Examine current child protection laws.
   1.4 Develop training curriculum. Material used in the course.
   1.5 Test training modules. Have a test group to validate all modules for accuracy.
   1.6 Validate curriculum. Ensure the final product is approved by the project management team.
   1.7 Publish curriculum. Publish to blackboard and print copies for class.
2. *Trained parents*
   2.1 Conduct cell phone dangers training. Provide material to parents and guardians.
   2.2 Conduct cell phone protection training with parental control features. Show iPhone and carrier safety features to audience. Provide smart cards to audience.
   2.3 Conduct parental involvement training. Allow audience to engage in practical application and role-play to ensure understanding.
3. *Project management*
   3.1 Form a project team. Make contact with potential team members.
   3.2 Propose and select a project. Discuss project options and select one that all team members agree on.
   3.3 Develop a project charter. Work on the project charter with team members.
   3.4 Develop a project plan. Create a plan with team members.
   3.5 Provide status report 1. Produce status report.
   3.6 Provide status report 2. Produce status report.
   3.7 Evaluate the project. Evaluate the project between team members.
   3.8 Report and record results. Submit revised and validated project for final grade.

Change Control System

A change control system is a collection of formal, documented procedures that define how project performance will be monitored and evaluated and includes the steps by which official project documents may be changed. It includes the paperwork, tracking systems, processes, and approval levels necessary for authorizing changes (PMBOK 2008).

Roles and Responsibilities

Organization Chart

The organization chart is a method for depicting inter-relationships among a group of persons working together toward a common objective. See Figure E.1.

Roles and Duties

Project roles and responsibilities must be assigned to project stakeholders who are actively involved in the work of the project, such as the project manager, other members of the project management team, and the individual contributors.

Project Manager (Jin Asato). The project manager is overall responsible for the project to include planning and defining the scope, activity planning and sequencing, resource planning and allocation, schedules, budget, cost estimates, and project documentation.

Training Developer (Jan Smith). The training developer is responsible for the entire training development plan to include curriculum or courseware development, classroom material development (e.g., handouts, exams), and media development (e.g., slide presentations).

Figure E.1 Organization chart depicts the reporting relationships

Trainer (Syd Green). The trainer is responsible for conducting all training to include classroom reservations, media tests, scheduling, rehearsing, instruction, and critiques.

Responsibility Matrix

It is a structure that relates the project organization breakdown structure to the work breakdown structure to help ensure that each component of the project's scope of work is assigned to a person or team. The responsible party for each activity in the work breakdown structure (WBS) is depicted in the responsibility matrix. See Figure E.2.

WBS\Person	Jin	Syd	Jan
Output 1.0 Published curriculum			
1.1 Determine training modules	S	A	R
1.2 Research application technologies	S	A	R
1.3 Research project legalities	S	A	R
1.4 Develop training curriculum	S	A	R
1.5 Test training modules	S	A	R
1.6 Validate curriculum	S	A	R
1.7 Publish curriculum	S	A	R
Output 2.0 Trained parents			
2.1 Conduct cell phone dangers training	S	R	A
2.2 Conduct cell phone protections training	S	R	A
2.3 Conduct parental involvement training	S	R	A
Output 3.0 Project management			
3.1 Form a project team	S	A	R
3.2 Propose and select a project	S	A	R
3.3 Develop a project charter	S	A	R
3.4 Develop a project plan	S	A	R
3.5 Provide status report 1	S	A	R
3.6 Provide status report 2	S	A	R
3.7 Evaluate the project	S	A	R
3.8 Report and record results	S	A	R

Responsible = R, Accountable = A, Sign-Off Required = S

Figure E.2 Responsibility matrix depicting the WBS

Schedule

Gantt Chart

Introduces and presents a matrix relating the project time frame to the outputs and activities of the WBS. See Figure E.3.

Network Diagram

Introduces and presents a project network diagram depicting the dependencies between the activities of the WBS. See Figure E.4.

Control

The project manager will be in charge of tracking the difference between the scheduled activities and actual activities. If a task is missing the schedule, the project manager will be responsible for determining whether the reason for missing the mark is acceptable or whether the resources and effort must be rebalanced to address the issue. Regardless of whether the variance is acceptable or not, they will be communicated to the stakeholders during the weekly project meeting.

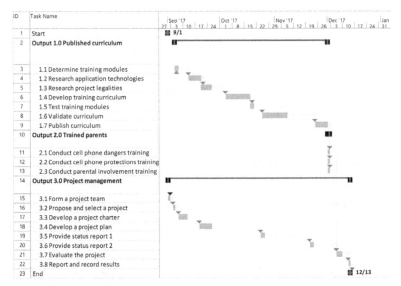

Figure E.3 Gantt chart

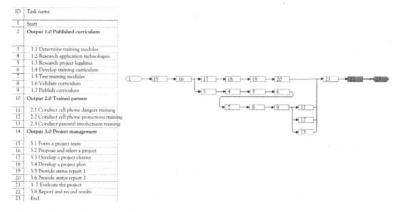

ID	Task name
1	Start
2	Output 1.0 Published curriculum
3	1.1 Determine training modules
4	1.2 Research application technologies
5	1.3 Research project legalities
6	1.4 Develop training curriculum
7	1.5 Test training modules
8	1.6 Validate curriculum
9	1.7 Publish curriculum
10	Output 2.0 Trained parents
11	2.1 Conduct cell phone dangers training
12	2.2 Conduct cell phone protections training
13	2.3 Conduct parental involvement training
14	Output 3.0 Project management
15	3.1 Form a project team
16	3.2 Propose and select a project
17	3.3 Develop a project charter
18	3.4 Develop a project plan
19	3.5 Provide status report 1
20	3.6 Provide status report 2
21	3. 7 Evaluate the project
22	3.8 Report and record results
23	End

Figure E.4 Network diagram

Budget

Budget by Output

The cost of the project can be tracked by activity. The total of all project activities for each output is shown in the subtotal column of the chart. This is shown in Table E.1.

Budget by Resources

The cost of the project can be broken down by resources. This is shown in Table E.2.

Resource Notes

The following is a listing of the base rates of each of the resources used in this project.

1. The base rate of the project manager is 45.00 U.S. dollars per hour.
2. The base rate of the training developer is 35.00 U.S. dollars per hour.
3. The base rate of the trainer is 25.00 U.S. dollars per hour.

Control

The project manager will be responsible for maintaining the budget. The hours will be recorded by individuals directly assigned in each activity

Table E.1 **Budget by output**

WBS		Actual cost	Subtotal
Output 1	**Published curriculum**		$6,845.00
	Activity 1.1 Determine training modules	$280.00	
	Activity 1.2 Research application technologies	$1,680.00	
	Activity 1.3 Research project legalities	$700.00	
	Activity 1.4 Develop training curriculum	$2,625.00	
	Activity 1.5 Test training modules	$360.00	
	Activity 1.6 Validate curriculum	$600.00	
	Activity 1.7 Publish curriculum	$600.00	
Output 2	**Trained parents**		$225.00
	Activity 2.1 Conduct cell phone dangers training	$75.00	
	Activity 2.2 Conduct cell phone protection training	$75.00	
	Activity 2.3 Conduct parental involvement training	$75.00	
Output 3	**Project management**		$10,245.00
	Activity 3.1 Form a project team	$135.00	
	Activity 3.2 Propose and select a project	$210.00	
	Activity 3.3 Develop a project charter	$4,200.00	
	Activity 3.4 Develop a project plan	$4,200.00	
	Activity 3.5 Provide a status report (#1)	$135.00	
	Activity 3.6 Provide a status report (#2)	$135.00	
	Activity 3.7 Evaluate the project	$1,050.00	
	Activity 3.8 Report and record results	$180.00	
Total			$17,315.00

and will be provided to the project manager weekly. The project manager will reconcile the budget weekly and submit a report to human resources during their weekly project meeting.

Table E.2 Budget by resources

Resource name	Baseline cost
Project manager	$ 4,725.00
Training developer	$ 9,415.00
Trainer	$ 2,925.00
Materials	$ 250.00
Total	$ 17,315.00

Subsidiary Management Plans

Subsidiary management plans, as depicted next, will be implemented and monitored by the project manager. The project commenced on September 15, 2017, and will be completed on December 08, 2017. The project status meetings will be held in the PL-12 classroom at predetermined dates and times per project plan.

Staffing Management Plan. The project manager will be responsible for presenting human resources with the following staff management plan information:

- Staff acquisition
- Resource calendars
- Training needs
- Recognition and rewards
- Compliance reports
- Safety reports

Communications Management Plan. The project manager will be responsible for reporting the weekly status of the project. Weekly status checks will be conducted and reported to the project manager for final review and approval. Additionally, the training developer will maintain constant communications with the project manager and trainer during the development process to ensure the appropriate content and resource allocations are applied and in accordance with the project management plan.

Risk Management Plan. All risks to the project will be immediately reported to the project manager who will evaluate the impact of the risk and determine whether it is acceptable to continue or how to apply additional resources to get the project back on track. The project manager will share the risk-mitigation plan with the team during their weekly status meeting to collectively access and discuss the potential risk of the project and determine the best course of action (accepting risk).

Training Development Plan. In cooperation with the project manager and trainer, the training development plan requires the training developer to develop and submit at least two drafts and a final training development plan for review by the entire team, then approved by the project manager before any publication or print of the training courseware.

Courseware Validation Plan. After making the necessary changes to the training development plan, the training developer will validate all courseware and publish it in the format specified by the trainer. Once published, the prescribed trainer can access the curriculum and begin training.

APPENDIX F

Example Model Application

CHAPTER 2

Macro Environment Analysis

2.1 Introduction

To start our analysis of moving Jimmy John's to Canada, we wanted to conduct a macroenvironment analysis to determine whether Canada would be a good country to internationalize to. Data is presented and analyzed using the PEST (political, economic, social, technological) model presented in Figure F.1.[1]

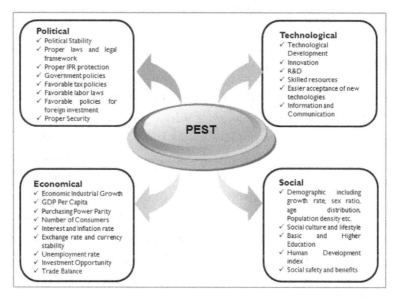

Figure F.1 PEST analysis tool

---

[1] CrackMBA PEST business analysis tool. This figure illustrates the elements of the PEST tool. Retrieved from http://crackmba.com/pest-analysis/

We chose to analyze the macroenvironment with the PEST model because the model allows us to analyze key environments that could make or break our internationalization of the franchise. It provides us with an overview of the business environment in Canada, identifies risks to minimize their impact of our internationalization, and discovers opportunities we previously did not see. All areas represented in Figure F.1 will not be used, only those deemed pertinent to opening a franchise of Jimmy John's Gourmet Sandwiches internationally.

2.2 Political Environment

2.2.1 Introduction

The political environment in Canada is an import factor in deciding to franchise Jimmy John's restaurant. What is the political stability, as well as the crime rate in Canada? Are there Government policies that will affect our franchise? These are just a few of the questions that we will address to determine whether Canada is an ideal country to start a Jimmy John's restaurant.

2.2.2 Political Stability

Canada has a large majority of provincial governments, which are of a different party than the majority federal government. Both federal and provincial governments have a wide range of authority under the Canadian constitution. It's doubtful at this point that any factional party could gain enough of a position anywhere in the country to cause much of a problem (Haddock 2014). Throughout the world, Canada is seen as a democracy. They have a constitutional monarchy; they have a party system and a federal system. The country just went through its major election. The Prime Minister, Justin Trudeau, was elected last year in November. He brings in a new era of liberal leadership after conservative Stephen Harper's near-decade in power.[2]

---

[2] http://www.foxnews.com/world/2015/11/03/trudeau-to-be-sworn-in-as-canada-new-prime-minister-after-nearly-decade.html

2.2.3 Proper Laws and Legal Framework

There is no pending legislation at this time that would affect our franchise of Jimmy John's Gourmet Sandwiches into the Canadian market.

2.2.4 Proper IPR Protection

The intellectual property of Jimmy John's restaurant will remain their property in accordance with their franchise guidance.

2.2.5 Government Policies

The only government policy that would affect us would be the language law in the province. This law enforces that the primary language in an establishment is French (Quebec 2016). As English is our first language, this will be an obstacle that we will have to overcome.

2.2.6 Favorable Tax Policies

Canada has a much lower corporate tax rate than the United States, 15 percent at the federal level plus another 11 percent on average from provincial corporate taxes. In the United States, there is a federal corporate tax rate of 35 percent plus an average state corporate tax rate of about 4 percent (McBride 2014). We will have to file for taxes in Canada, as well as the United States. However, we would be able to submit for a tax credit (McBride 2014).

2.2.7 Favorable Labor Laws

They are no favorable laws that would affect the nature of this venture.

2.2.8 Favorable Policies for Foreign Investment

We will have to abide by the food safety and proper labeling regulations. This is an important concern for Canadians. Labeling standards for food products help make sure that consumers have the information they need about the food they are purchasing. Any item we plan on packaging, distributing, or selling food products in Canada must meet labeling standards (Business 2016).

The following was pulled from the Canadian government's web page on corporate social responsibility:

> The Government of Canada has in place a variety of initiatives which demonstrate Canada's longstanding commitment to promoting responsible business practice. Through its actions, the Government facilitates the commercial success of Canadian companies active abroad while enhancing the contribution of their activities to the broad economic growth of Canada and its trading partners, including those with developing and emergent economies. We work with the Canadian business community, civil society organizations, foreign governments and communities, as well as other stakeholders to foster and promote responsible business practices, and thus support sustainable economic growth and shared value.

2.2.9 Proper Security

Crime in Canada is an important factor in establishing a Jimmy John's restaurant. According to the police-reported crime statistics in Canada, in 2014, the crime rate in Canada continued to go down with the homicide rate declining to the lowest level in the last 46 years. The crime severity rate also went down by 3 percent. Observers claim that one of the reasons for this decline is the tightening of crime laws by conservative legislators (Boyce 2015). In 2014, both the police-reported Crime Severity Index (CSI) and the crime rate continued to decline in Canada. This is the premise of a longer-term downward trend. While the majority of violations decreased in 2014, the overall decline in the severity of crime was primarily the result of fewer incidents of breaking and entering, as well as robbery (Boyce 2015). All other provinces and territories, with the exception of Yukon, British Columbia, and Alberta, recorded a decline in their CSI between 2013 and 2014. Despite overall declines, several CMAs recorded an increase in their CSI in 2014 (Boyce 2015).

In 2014, extortion, sexual violations against children, and abduction were among the few violent offences to record an increase, while almost all other violent violations decreased and the rate of homicide remained stable. Also, in 2014, the youth CSI continued to decline. Decreases in youth CSI were recorded in all provinces and territories, with the exception of Yukon. Declines were seen in the majority of offences, including all forms of property crime and most forms of violent crime (Boyce 2015).

2.2.10 Conclusion

In conclusion, the political environment of Canada is ideal for this venture. A government with a democratic base that is as stable as the United States is less worry of a drastic political change. The crime rate is in a downward trend in almost all of the provinces. The taxes for the franchise would be submitted in both countries. However, we will be able to claim a tax break in the United States for revenue earned in Canada. The Canadian government is big on labeling all ingredients in the food industry. This will not be a problem with all of the ingredients that are used to make Jimmy John's Gourmet Sandwiches.

2.3 Economic Environment

Removed text

2.4 Social Environment

Removed text

2.5 Technological Environment

Removed text

2.6 Conclusion

Our conclusion, after the completion of the initial PEST macroenvironment analysis, there are no identified risks, and there are many opportunities to internationalizing Jimmy John's Gourmet Sandwiches. The political environment of Canada is ideal for this venture. There democratic government is as stable as the United States, and though there are taxes to be paid in both countries, we would get a tax break in the U.S. crime is going down in Canada, and there were no barriers identified with Jimmy John's Gourmet Sandwiches ingredients. Canada's economic environment is in a good position. Canada's economy has not been a top performer, but it has also not done poorly either; it has remained stable in the midst of the volatile global economy. The analysis of the social factors identified one area of caution in relation to the diminishing class lines between the middle class and working class. However, other businesses have continued to be successful in Canada, despite the class structure, and as addressed in the economic environment, Canada has remained stable. The spoken language is the same in Canada as in the United States. The population and age structure prove to be similar as well as Canada's business etiquette to the United States. The social similarities between Canada and the United States make it a great location to open the first international franchise. From the technology standpoint, Canada is more than capable to cover any requirements that Jimmy John's would need. There is not a high standard for technological skills or equipment in the fast food industry. With Jimmy John's, our specialty is fresh and fast. Now is the time to internationalize the Jimmy John's Gourmet Sandwiches franchise into Canada, and we are the investors to do it.

APPENDIX G

Example of a Progress Report

Project/Task Update

With today's technology and information literally at the tips of our fingers, we need to educate ourselves, so we can keep our children as safe as possible while utilizing the tools and features that cell phones have to offer. All it takes is one wrong word in a search engine or one wrong push of the screen and a child can end up with information they should not be privy to. The goal of keeping children safe is going to be accomplished by educating parents with the tools and skills necessary to accomplish the goal. Our outputs of published curriculum, trained parents, and project management are what we will utilize to ensure we continue to stay on track to achieve the purpose of educating parents. All purposes are still achievable.

With the conclusion of status report two, the project is currently within budget. Activities 1.6 from output 1 and 3.6 from output 3 that were completed during this reporting period were on target with the planned and baseline cost set from the initiating phase of the project.

Activities 1.6 (validate curriculum) under output 1 (published curriculum) and 3.6 (provide status report#2) under output 3 (project management) under the current reporting period. We are currently working ahead of schedule with 25 percent for activity 1.7 (publish curriculum). The next reporting period will include the rest of the activities for output 1.3 to include the start through end of output 2 (trained parents).

For the next reporting period, we will have completed output 1 (published curriculum) and output 2 (trained parents). We will be working on our final evaluation of the project followed by concluding the project. All project tasks are either on time or ahead of schedule.

Schedule

Tracking the Gantt chart with baseline and updated actual taskbars. See Figure G.1.

Budget

By Output: Planned to Actual

It is the budget by output with baseline, planned, and actual cost, with variance. See Table G.1.

By Resource: Planned to Actual

It is the budget by resource with baseline, planned, and actual cost, with variance. Please see Table G.2.

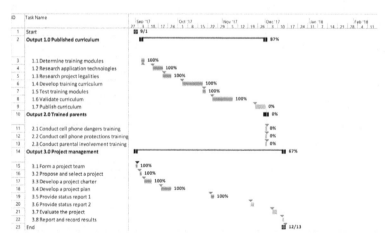

Figure G.1 Tracking Gantt

Table G.1 *Budget by output*

WBS		Baseline cost ($)		Actual cost ($)		Planned cost ($)		Cost variance ($)	
		Cost	Subtotal	Cost	Subtotal	Cost	Subtotal	Costs variance	Subtotal
Output 1	Published curriculum		6,845		7,120		7,720		875
	Activity 1.1 Determine training modules	280		280		280		0	
	Activity 1.2 Research application	1,680		1,680		1,680		0	
	Activity 1.3 Research project legalities	700		1,120		1,120		420	
	Activity 1.4 Develop training curriculum	2,625		3,080		3,080		455	
	Activity 1.5 Test training modules	360		360		360		0	
	Activity 1.6 Validate curriculum	600		600		600		0	
	Activity 1.7 Publish curriculum	600		0		600		0	
Output 2	Trained parents		225		0		225		0
	Activity 2.1 Conduct cell phone dangers	75		0		75		0	
	Activity 2.2 Conduct cell phone protection	75		0		75		0	
	Activity 2.3 Conduct parental involvement	75		0		75		0	

(Continued)

Table G.1 Budget by output   (Continued)

WBS		Baseline cost ($)		Actual cost ($)		Planned cost ($)		Cost variance ($)	
		Cost	Subtotal	Cost	Subtotal	Cost	Subtotal	Costs variance	Subtotal
	Project management		10,245		9,015		10,245		0
	Activity 3.1 Form project team	135		135		135		0	
	Activity 3.2 Propose and select a project	210		210		210		0	
	Activity 3.3 Develop project charter	4,200		4,200		4,200		0	
Output 3	Activity 3.4 Develop project plan	4,200		4,200		4,200		0	
	Activity 3.5 Provide status report (#1)	135		135		135		0	
	Activity 3.6 Provide status report (#2)	135		135		135		0	
	Activity 3.7 Evaluate project	1,050		0		1,050		0	
	Activity 3.8 Report and record results	180		0		180		0	
Total			17,315		16,135		18,190		875

Table G.2 Budget by resource

Name	Baseline cost (in U.S. dollars)	Planned cost (in U.S. dollars)	Actual cost (in U.S. dollars)	Cost variance (in U.S. dollars)
Project manager	4,725.00	4,725.00	4,095.00	0.00
Training developer	9,415.00	10,290.00	9,590.00	875.00
Trainer	2,925.00	2,925.00	2,450.00	0.00
Materials	250.00	250.00	0.00	0.00
Total	17,315.00	18,190.00	16,135.00	875.00

APPENDIX H

Examples of Lessons Learned

Project Summary

Project Purpose

With today's technology and information literally at the tips of our fingers, we need to educate ourselves, so we can keep our children as safe as possible while utilizing the tools and features that cell phones have to offer. All it takes is one wrong word in a search engine or one wrong push of the screen and a child can end up with information they should not be privy to. The goal of keeping children safe is going to be accomplished by educating parents with the tools and skills necessary to accomplish the goal. Our outputs of published curriculum, trained parents, and project management are what we will utilize to ensure we continue to stay on track to achieve the purpose of educating parents. All purposes are still achievable.

End of Project Status

With the conclusion of the final evaluation, Outputs 1 and 2 have been completed as scheduled. Output 1 had a small variance in activities 1.3 (research project legalities) and 1.4 (develop training curriculum) due to additional legal research that had to be performed. Output 2 has been completed within budget and on time. Output 3 is just pending the completion of activity 3.8 (report and record results), which is also expected to be completed within budget and on time.

Project Impact

Numerous individuals on the job have been complaining about their inability to keep their kids safe on cell phones. We conducted a survey and determined over 95 percent of the children from coworkers had iPhones.

Based off the study, our team developed and implemented a training program covering iPhone, application, and some Internet safeties. We also addressed the issue of trust and communication. We reached 93 percent of the workers due to some being on mission or leave status. Overall, the impact was well received, and based off feedback, most parents have taken an active role in their child's cell phone lives. A complete 100 percent product was completed and presented to the learners. Effective training had a positive impact on the primary stakeholders of the parents and children. Training developers created an outstanding product that was delivered by the trainer.

Recommendations

Future projects would be to expand safeties from phones to mobile devices, computers and even television products. Televisions are now Smart TVs and have all kinds of access to online applications. Protecting children and educating parents would take extensive research for proper application and settings that could be universal based on setting, or at least get parents comfortable researching how to set their devices up to keep the children as safe as possible.

Project Schedule

Significant Dates and Events

On September 01, 2017, we started our project. From there, we started and completed our project management from September 01 to December 08, 2017. Concurrently, we developed and published our curriculum from September 08 to November 27, 2017. Trainers conducted our outstanding training on November 28, and we intend on closing our project on December 08, 2017.

Planned to Actual

Output 1 had a small variance in activities 1.3 (research project legalities) and 1.4 (develop training curriculum) due to additional legal research that had to be performed.

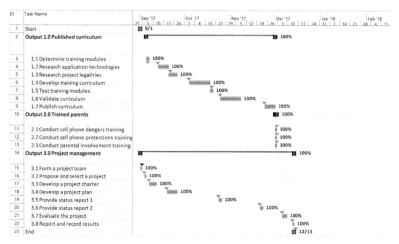

Figure H.1 Tracking Gantt chart

Tracking Gantt Chart

Present a tracking Gantt chart showing planned and actual activities. See Figure H.1.

Project Budget

Funding

The source of funding for this project was the U.S. Government (Department of Defense). The estimated cost for this entire project was initially estimated at 17,315 U.S. dollars, but the actual cost was 18,190 U.S. dollars, which leaves a cost variance of 875 U.S. dollars.

Subcontractors

There was one subcontractor for this project (trainer) who was paid a total of 2,925 U.S. dollars for the entirety of the contract upon completion of training.

Planned to Actual

Variances to the budget for activities and the overall project were as follows:

1. Research project legalities.
   a. Baseline: 700 U.S. dollars
   b. Actual: 1,120 U.S. dollars
   c. Cost variance: 420 U.S. dollars
2. Training curriculum development.
   a. Baseline: 2,625 U.S. dollars
   b. Actual: 3,080 U.S. dollars
   c. Cost variance: 455 U.S. dollars
3. Total cost variance: 875 U.S. dollars

Budget by Output

The budget by output with baseline, planned, and actual cost, with variance.

See Table H.1.

Budget by Resources

The budget by resource with baseline, planned, and actual cost, with variance. See Table H.2.

Lessons Learned

Our project was pretty straightforward due to the fact that the training was being submitted for another college class. This reduced the risk of incompleteness as to not fail another class.

Project Initiation and Planning

One lesson learned was being more familiar with MS Project and its intricacies. For example, the cumulative cost curve had to be done via Excel due to MS Projects compilation of the data. Another was looking for small indentations that caused the data to be off.

Project Executing and Closing

The training went over with great reviews. One issue was the trainer went a little long in a couple of sections that made the training go long. However, the training was still conducted in one day, and we actually

Table H.1 Budget by output

WBS		Baseline cost ($)		Actual cost ($)		Planned cost ($)		Cost variance ($)	
		Cost	Subtotal	Cost	Subtotal	Cost	Subtotal	Costs variance	Subtotal
	Published curriculum		6,845		7,720		7,720		875
Output 1	Activity 1.1 Determine training modules	280		280		280		0	
	Activity 1.2 Research application	1,680		1,680		1,680		0	
	Activity 1.3 Research project legalities	700		1,120		1,120		420	
	Activity 1.4 Develop training curriculum	2,625		3,080		3,080		455	
	Activity 1.5 Test training modules	360		360		360		0	
	Activity 1.6 Validate curriculum	600		600		600		0	
	Activity 1.7 Publish curriculum	600		600		600		0	
Output 2	Trained parents		225		225		225		0
	Activity 2.1 Conduct cell phone dangers	75		75		75		0	
	Activity 2.2 Conduct cell phone protection	75		75		75		0	
	Activity 2.3 Conduct parental involvement	75		75		75		0	

(Continued)

Table H.1 *Budget by output*   (Continued)

WBS		Baseline cost ($)		Actual cost ($)		Planned cost ($)		Cost variance ($)	
		Cost	Subtotal	Cost	Subtotal	Cost	Subtotal	Costs variance	Subtotal
	Project management		10,245		10,065		10,245		0
	Activity 3.1 Form project team	135		135		135		0	
	Activity 3.2 Propose and select a project	210		210		210		0	
	Activity 3.3 Develop project charter	4,200		4,200		4,200		0	
Output 3	Activity 3.4 Develop project plan	4,200		4,200		4,200		0	
	Activity 3.5 Provide status report (#1)	135		135		135		0	
	Activity 3.6 Provide status report (#2)	135		135		135		0	
	Activity 3.7 Evaluate project	1,050		1,050		1,050		0	
	Activity 3.8 Report and record results	180		0		180		0	
Total			17,315		18,010		18,190		875

Table H.2 Budget by resources

Name	Baseline cost (in U.S. dollars)	Planned cost (in U.S. dollars)	Actual cost (in U.S. dollars)	Cost variance(in U.S. dollars)
Project manager	4,725.00	4,725.00	4,545.00	0.00
Training developer	9,415.00	10,290.00	10,290.00	875.00
Trainer	2,925.00	2,925.00	2,925.00	0.00
Materials	250.00	250.00	250.00	0.00
Total	17,315.00	18,190.00	18,010.00	875.00

conducted a second training later in the week to pick up stragglers that did not attend.

Project Management

The project was successfully completed. However, some of the challenges faced involved time, cost, and communications. Due to work and additionally responsibilities outside of this project, it was critical that enough time was set aside on all of our schedules to be able to meet and discuss project changes and updates throughout the project timeline. Google Drive was essential in helping us have a central location to upload updated material. It also allowed us to engage in group chat to remain up to date on the changes and updates made to the project management documents.

Cost factor fluctuated due to additional research that had to be performed due to the changing nature of the technology front in regard to cell phones. Finally, sometimes, there was miscommunication when it came to version controlling. However, that was fixed after attention was brought to it.

The following project management knowledge areas will describe our evaluation and how we were able to initiate, plan, execute, monitor, and control, and then, close this project:

1. *Integration.* By following the project management process, our project team successfully developed and integrated the project charter, the project management plan, directed and managed project work, monitored and controlled the project while performing integrated change control, and then, closed the project by phase and by output.

2. *Scope.* During the planning phase of the project management process as it relates to project scope, our project team defined the scope of our project, planned a scope management plan, collected project requirements, and then created a work breakdown structure (WBS) to allocate the project scope workload within the team as it applied to the project management plan. Additionally, during the monitoring and controlling phase, our project manager validated and controlled the scope of the project.

3. *Time.* Also, during the planning phase of the project management process as it relates to time, our project team defined our activities, sequenced these activities, estimated resources and duration, planned a scope management plan, and then developed a schedule to capture and timetable our project activities. Also, during the monitoring and controlling phase, our project manager monitored and controlled the schedule to keep the project on track. As a result, this project was always on or ahead of schedule throughout the process.

4. *Cost.* As it relates to cost during the planning phase of the project management process, our project team planned how we would manage project expenses, then calculated and estimated project costs, and then, developed a project budget. During the monitoring and controlling phase of the project management process, the project manager effectively controlled costs and kept the project on budget. At no time did we ever exceed our overall project budget, nor did we have to deviate from our budget allocations to cover shortfalls from other outputs.

5. *Quality.* During the planning phase of the project management process as it relates to quality, our team developed a quality management plan, performed quality assurance during the execution phase, and then, efficiently controlled quality during the monitoring and controlling phase.

6. *Human resources.* As it applies to human resources during the planning phase of the project management process, our team developed a human resources management plan to determine what human capital it would take to complete this project successfully. Then, during the execution phase, we acquired, developed, and managed our project team to perfection.

7. *Communications.* Just like the previous knowledge area, a communications management plan was developed first during the planning phase of the project management process, followed by managing communications in our project team during the execution phase of the project, and then, controlling communications during the monitoring and controlling phase. This team communicated with each other efficiently and effectively throughout the project lifecycle, and at no time did we need intervention by the project manager to mitigate a dispute.

8. *Risk.* Managing risk is sometimes complicated when undertaking a project, but in this project, our risk was directly associated with our outputs and was a simple training project that only required curriculum development, training, and project management to see it to completion. There was not much risk associated with this project other than human resources, budget, and time, which were never a problem for this project. Our team did so by following the project management process starting with the planning phase. In this particular phase, our project team developed a risk management plan encompassing all identified risks, and then, performing a risk analysis and risk-based decision scenarios to have some canned risk responses if needed. Like all knowledge areas, our project manager controlled all residual risk during the monitoring and controlling phase of the project management process, and we never had to mitigate risk.

9. *Procurement.* Procurement as a knowledge area was planned, conducted, controlled, and closed by phase during the project management process. Our procurement of training materials and equipment to conduct the training was provided by the government because this was a government training plan and did not require and project resources in regards to procurement.

Follow-Up

As this was the first time that this curriculum was delivered, I would allot one more day of training to allow for more learner interaction. I would also get the training developer to explore the options of applications that parents could use as a quick reference guide that could be followed during the training lecture.

APPENDIX I

Example Literature Review

The course theme for a research project was identified as the African continent. Within this theme, student teams had freedom to define their own project focus. One group decided to do research on the adoption of banking with a focus on culture. Their literature review contained sections on (a) banking adoption, (b) culture, (c) culture and business, and (d) summary. These sections are presented as follows.

Banking Adoption

Limited research exists as to why consumers adopt formal bank accounts. Current efforts to identify reasons for adopting bank accounts either focus on individual country case studies or cross-country comparisons. In an individual country case, Owusu–Frimpong (199) found that Ghanaian consumer valued efficient service, understanding (of product features), and high rates of interest when opening accounts. In Ghana, personal influence from friends and relatives, opinion of leaders, and the trustworthiness of the source are very important. In a cross-country comparison, Blankson, Omar, and Cheng (2009) took this a step further by exploring student adoption reasons between developed and developing countries. In a survey of students from the United States and Ghana, they concluded that adoption reasons were not significantly different. The primary determining factors were convenience, competence, recommendation by parents, and free banking.

As important as it is to understand why consumers may choose to adopt banking, several compelling research efforts focused on the key obstacles to banking adoption. Using information from 209 banks in 62 countries, Beck, Demirguc-Kunt, and Peria (2008) identified several constraining barriers. Specifically, minimum balances for checking accounts, annual fees, and document requirements, associated with these accounts, the number of delivery channels for lending products, minimum amounts for consumer loans relative to GDP per capita, and days to process consumer loans seem to constitute true hurdles to accessing formal banking services.

Most recently, the World Bank began to expand research into these obstacles in an attempt to understand the extent of financial inclusion and the degree to which such groups as the poor, women, and youth are excluded from formal financial systems (Demirguc-Kunt and Klapper 2012). This research effort culminated in the creation of the Global Financial Inclusion (Global Findex) Database that measures how adults in 148 economies save, borrow, make payments, and manage risk. The indicators are culled from survey data gleaned from interviews with more than 150,000 nationally representative and randomly selected adults aged 15 years and above.

Demirguc-Kunt and Klapper (2013) define an account at a formal financial institution (% age 15+) as follows: *The percentage of respondents with an account (self or together with someone else) at a bank, credit union, another financial institution (e.g., cooperative, microfinance institution), or the post office (if applicable) including respondents who reported having a debit card.*

The identified barriers to financial inclusion by examining cross-country data on self-reported reasons do not having a formal account. Those self-reported reasons are described in Table I.1.

It could be argued that the top barriers such as *not enough money, too expensive,* and *too far away* would not be as prevalent in higher-income

Table I.1 Self-reported barriers to use of formal accounts

Barrier description	Percentage
Not enough money	30
Too expensive	25
Family member already has account	23
Too far away	20
Lack of necessary documentation	18
Lack of trust	13
Religious reasons	5

Source: Demirguc-Kunt and Klapper (2012).

nations as in lower-income nations. In fact, emphasizing the disparity between the have and have-not countries, Demirguc-Kunt and Klapper (2013) state that

> Analysis of Global Findex data shows that account penetration is higher in economies with higher national income as measured by GDP per capita, confirming the findings of previous studies. But national income explains much less of the variation in account penetration for low- and lower-middle-income economies (Demirguc-Kunt, and Klapper 2013, p. 3).

Later, they indicate that income has a weak correlation to the adoption of banking in those nations with 2,200 U.S. dollars GDP per capita or less, which comprise the bottom 50 percent of the income distribution (Demirguc-Kunt and Klapper 2013, p. 12).

Given the self-reported nature of these responses, one is compelled to investigate whether there is a common national undercurrent or theme, outside of income, that would help explain the reason for the barriers. As the top barriers might evaporate in developed countries due to higher income, could the other barriers such as required documentation, trust, family, and religion be grouped into a consistent theme? Inglehart and Baker (2000) noted that "economic development seems to have a powerful impact on cultural values: the value systems of rich countries differ systematically from those of poor countries" (Inglehart and Baker 2000, p. 29). Employing this thought, one could argue that cultural values may have a different effect on banking adoption rates when comparing higher-income nations with lower-income nations.

Culture

Related to culture, Hofstede (1980) defines national culture as "the collective mental programming of the people in a national context." Hofstede undertook a factor analysis of responses to questions relating to workplace issues and proposed that attitudes, beliefs, and behaviors could be categorized into four cultural dimensions. The four dimensions are individualism–collectivism, masculinity–femininity, power distance, and uncertainty avoidance.

Several years later, a fifth dimension was added (Hofstede and Bond 1988) as a result of studying explosive growth in East Asia. Hofstede and Bond determined that the original four dimensions of culture did not correlate to the growth in East Asia economies. Researchers utilized a modified questionnaire called the Chinese Value Survey (CVS) that controlled for cultural nuances and attempted to eliminate Western bias in the survey process (Hofstede and Minkov 2010). A statistical analysis of the CVS results identified a similar (but slightly different) four dimensions to Hofstede's original work. Specifically, three of four dimensions correlated with the exception of uncertainty avoidance: it had no equivalent in the CVS survey. On a more positive note, through use of the improved survey, researchers identified a new cultural element titled Confucian Dynamism. Confucian Dynamism (Hofstede and Bond 1988) was coined from the ideas of Confucius, which centered on dynamic, future-oriented mentalities versus static, tradition-oriented mentalities, or put another way: long-term versus short-term orientation.

A sixth dimension—indulgence—was described by Hofstede (2010) as, "observed national differences in happiness." The dimension is measured by asking people how satisfied they are with their lives and how happy they feel.

Hofstede's overall six dimensions are summarized in Table I.2.

Another often-cited researcher on the topic of national culture is Trompenaars (1994). Employing a research approach similar to Hofstede's, Trompenaars identified five relationship orientations that account for how people in different cultures relate in the work place. Trompenaars' orientations are:

- Universalism versus particularism
- Individualism versus communitarianism
- Neutral versus emotionalism
- Specific versus diffuse
- Achievement versus ascription

Although both Hofstede and Trompenaars utilized similar research approaches in methodology and survey audience selection and concluded with five variables, the only cultural overlap appears to be related to the

Table I.2 Hofstede's six cultural dimensions

Dimension	Explanation
Individualism–collectivism	Individualism pertains to societies in which the ties between individuals are loose: everyone is expected to look after him- or herself and his or her immediate family.
	Collectivism as its opposite pertains to societies in which people from birth onward are integrated into strong, cohesive in-groups, which throughout people's lifetime continue to protect them in exchange for unquestioning loyalty (Hofstede 2010, p. 92)
Masculinity–femininity	A society is called masculine when emotional gender roles are clearly distinct: men are supposed to be assertive, tough, and focused on material success, whereas women are supposed to be more modest, tender, and concerned with the quality of life. A society is called feminine when emotional gender roles overlap: both men and women are supposed to be modest, tender, and concerned with the quality of life (Hofstede 2010, p. 140)
Power distance	The extent to which the less powerful members of institutions and organizations within a country expect and accept that power is distributed unequally (Hofstede 2010, p. 61)
Uncertainty avoidance	The extent to which the members of a culture feel threatened by ambiguous or unknown situations. This feeling is, among other manifestations, expressed through nervous stress and in a need for predictability: a need for written and unwritten rules (Hofstede 2010, p. 191)
Long-term orientation	The fostering of virtues oriented toward future rewards—in particular, perseverance and thrift. Its opposite pole, short-term orientation, stands for the fostering of virtues related to the past and present—in particular, respect for tradition, preservation of *face*, and fulfilling social obligations (Hofstede 2010, p. 230)
Indulgence	A tendency to allow relatively free gratification of basic and natural human desires related to enjoying life and having fun. Its opposite pole, restraint, reflects a conviction that such gratification needs to be curbed and regulated by strict social norms (Hofstede 2010, p. 281)

Source: Hofstede (2010).

concept of individualism versus collectivism. In addition, the variables do not have practical relevance to a decision to bank.

In addition to specific debate about varying culture factors, the literature places emphasis on the concept of trust. Most perspectives on trust establish that risk is required for trust to influence choice and behavior (Lewis and Weigert 1985). The source of risk is generally related to the uncertainty level associated with an outcome. Echoing that, Luhmann (1979) stated that, "a fundamental condition of trust is that it must be possible for the partner to abuse the trust."

Aside from skepticism about others in a transaction, the literature indicates that other perspectives of trust emphasize mutually fulfilling relationships. Larzelere and Huston (1980) propose two qualities of trust: benevolence and honesty. Fukuyama and Ikenberry (1996) view trust as the expectation of regular, honest, and cooperative behavior based on commonly shared norms and values. Trust is a feeling of security, based primarily on the belief that one party's behavior is guided by favorable intentions toward the best interests of the other, and secondly, on the competence of a business to keep its promises (Delgado-Ballester and Munuera-Alerman 2001).

General surveys, such as the World Values Survey, assess trust by asking questions related to expectations about people in general and a country's institutions (Johnson and Mislin 2012). The trust measure of the World Values Survey has been noted as a measure that indicates an overall degree of trust, rather than directed at particular targets (Bhardwaj, Dietz, and Beamish 2007). Although trust may form in a variety of ways, whether and how trust is established depend on the societal norms and values that guide people's behavior and beliefs (Hofstede 1980). This implies that the choice of an individual to trust or not is heavily dependent on a nation's culture.

Culture and Business

Determining which cultural dimensions are most relevant to a consumer's choice to bank was challenging, given the available research literature. Although no previous research was found connecting culture to consumer banking choices, the literature does link national culture to certain aspects of banking. For instance, Kanagaretnam, Chee Yeow, and Lobo (2014) studied how differences in the national culture affect accounting conservatism and bank risk-taking. They focused on two dimensions of culture identified by Hofstede, individualism (IND) and uncertainty avoidance (UA). Using bank results from over 70 countries, they determined that banks in low IND and high UA societies report earnings more conservatively than banks in high IND and low UA societies. Conservative reporting means recognizing losses in a timelier manner, recognizing larger and timelier loan loss provisions, recognizing proportionally larger loan loss allowances, and recognizing larger and timelier loan charge-offs. Although the analysis was interesting, given that it applied to bank accounting practices at an enterprise level, it is not entirely applicable for our study of consumer choice in banking.

Kwok and Tadesse (2006) also draw conclusions between aspects of national culture and financial systems. They utilized Hofstede's uncertainty avoidance culture dimension as a measure of a country's propensity to select a market-based system versus a banking system. They concluded that countries characterized by higher uncertainty avoidance are more likely to have a bank-based system. Although the study relates national culture to a banking system selection, it does so at the country level, not at the consumer level.

In a related study, Bhardwaj, Dietz, and Beamish (2007) demonstrated the effect of a host country's culture on foreign direct investment (FDI) across 43 countries around the world, comprising 90 percent of the world's economy. Two cultural aspects were used, Hofstede's dimension of uncertainty avoidance and a measure of trust based on the World Values Survey. A number of variables that also affect FDI were controlled, including key economic, human capital, and governance infrastructure. Using statistical tests, the authors conclude that uncertainty avoidance has a significant and primary effect on FDI (lower uncertainty avoidance increases FDI), and that trust has a partial and secondary effect (higher trust increases FDI). Interestingly, it is also shown that an interactive effect plays a significant role, in that low uncertainty avoidance reduces the effect of trust on FDI. In other words, certain cultural values may take precedence or *trump* other cultural values in some situations. The authors suggest that "future research might specifically address the effects of culture on other facets of national competitiveness" (Bhardwaj, Dietz, and Beamish 2007, p. 46).

Everdingen and Waarts (2003) used five of Hofstede's dimensions to test the effect of a firm's adoption of innovative technology. Primary data in the form of 2,647 survey responses from various firms throughout 10 European countries regarding their adoption of IT system innovations were used to test hypotheses on these effects. They concluded that "higher levels of the uncertainty avoidance, masculinity and power distance dimensions in a country negatively influenced ERP adoption, while higher levels of long-term orientation have a significant positive influence" (Everdingen and Waarts 2003, p. 230). While not completely analogous, in the developing world, the decision to bank or not, where few opportunities have existed in the past, in many ways resembles the adoption of a new innovation. Note that, of Hofstede's cultural dimensions (five at the time of the study), the most significant influence was from long-term orientation.

Summary

A consumer's decision to bank is influenced by a variety of factors, framed as both advantages and obstacles. Demirguc-Kunt and Klapper (2013) offer a compelling study to analyze further. They report survey results indicating the main reasons that consumers choose not to bank (Table I.1) and report that adoption rates are higher in high-income economies than in lower-income economies. They also show that large variation in banking adoption for the low-income nations is not explained by low income alone.

Five of the seven self-reported reasons in the study (money, expense, family relation, proximity, and documentation) would likely be more of an obstacle in lower-income economies and less so for those with higher incomes. Aside from these major obstacles, what else may explain the variation in banking adoption? Might culture play a significant role? In the low-income countries, are these cultural factors somehow hidden behind the known major barriers, yet still underlie a fundamental reason for choosing not to bank? In the high-income nations, with the major barriers removed, do cultural factors have more *freedom*, in effect playing a more significant role? No study was found in the literature that specifically addresses these questions; therefore, our investigation aims to fill this gap and contribute to the understanding of factors that affect consumer utilization of financial institutions.

The literature points to utilizing one of Hofstede's cultural dimensions as a measurement for culture as it effects the consumer's decision to bank. Literature suggests that IND, UA, and long-term orientation (LTO) may be applicable. Although not much literature surrounds LTO as it is a more recent concept, it is an intriguing factor. Related to LTO and the concept of thrift, Hofstede (2010) indicated,

> the values at the LTO pole support entrepreneurial activity. Persistence (perseverance), or tenacity in the pursuit of whatever goals one has set, is an essential asset for a beginning entrepreneur... Thrift leads to savings and to availability of capital for reinvestment by oneself or one's relatives (Hofstede 2010, p. 243).

The literature indicates that trust is associated with situations where the uncertainty of outcomes and risk are involved, where there exists the possibility of abuse of that trust, as in the case of choosing to bank. The World Values Survey trust measure provides an indicator of the general level of cultural trust in each nation.

LTO's link to thrift and innovation make the measurement relevant for banking and lead us to hypothesize:

Hypothesis 1: Higher levels of a nation's LTO measure are associated with a higher consumer use of formal financial institutions.

Furthermore, the link between cultural trust and the decision to bank leads us to our second hypothesis:

Hypothesis 2: Higher levels of a nation's trust cultural measure are associated with a higher consumer use of formal financial institutions.

Finally, in an attempt to explain the differences between lower-income and higher-income economies, our third hypothesis is:

Hypothesis 3: LTO and trust will have a stronger effect on a consumer's use of formal financial institutions in higher-income nations than in lower-income nations.

Example Methodology Discussion

The theme of a course was the global adoption of solar energy. Within this overall theme, a student team did research on the factors that influence the adoption of solar power technology by households. During the literature review, the group discussed theories on the adoption of technology, and based upon this, identified a range of variables. The team decided to collect data by means of a survey to test the identified relationships between these variables and the adoption of solar energy. Their methodology section is provided as follows.

> A survey was produced to measure the factors that influenced inquiring consumers to adopt or not adopt solar energy technology for their home. The main reason the survey is relevant is its ability to obtain an aggregate insight on consumers' attitudes toward influences on household solar energy use. This insight can then be compared to analyze the relationships of consumers' perceptual attitudes with known facts about solar technology, as well as the impact social influences have on their adoption decision. The data being collected relied on the following assumptions:
>
> - Respondents are representative of the population being estimated, are willing to respond, and are honest in their responses.
> - They are not biased by conflicts of interest, such as employment with a solar energy company, or a competing form of renewable energy.

- Respondents are only allowed to complete the survey once.
- Data is normally distributed.
- The analyses selected are sufficient for the study to detect significant relationships between variables.
- Variables are clearly defined and are measurable.

Pretesting of this survey by 20 respondents unrelated to the research project has been performed to help ensure these assumptions are valid. The following sections will describe the method of data collection, define the variables being analyzed and the hypotheses being tested, and describe the methods of testing the data obtained.

Sample Collection

Self-administered surveys were distributed in two formats—printed and electronic—to consumers who currently use domestic solar energy technology, as well as those who inquired about it, yet chose not to use it. Due to time and budget constraints, samples were geographically limited to within the Spokane and neighboring areas. This limits the sample's representativeness of the U.S. population. Participating solar panel installation companies assisted in data collection by distributing surveys to the described consumers. To collect electronic surveys, e-mails containing a link to the survey were sent to consumers, which were collected instantaneously upon completion using Qualtrics survey software. Printed surveys were received via standard mail or fax machine and hand-tabulated. People who live in or near Spokane County, Washington, in the United States are potential participants. Surveys were distributed on November 19, 2012. Collection of surveys was completed November 30, 2012 in order to provide sufficient time for tabulation and analysis.

Sample Size

The following formula was used to estimate the number of responses needed to represent the survey. Due to time constraints and the limited scope of respondents surveyed, a fair amount of error has been allowed in order to limit the number of surveys needed to be a representative proportion of the population.

$$n = \frac{Z^2 \; \pi(1-\pi)}{e^2}$$

90% confidence (Z = 1.645)

0.2: indicates an estimated 20 percent response rate

e= error = 0.1: indicates that 10 percent of error on either side of the mean was allowed

n= 43

In other words, at least 43 responses were needed in order to fully represent the population, given the current allowed amount of error in the data.

Dependent Variable

Adoption rate of household solar power systems is the only dependent variable in this study. As the purpose of this study is determining what factors impact the adoption rate of solar power technology for household use in different nations around the world, the study focuses on the adoption rate of solar power systems as dependent on the various attitudinal and social influence variables. The definition of adoption rate in this research is the number of households that currently have solar panels installed to power some or all of its energy needs. This adoption rate was measured in a small geographic location, in a limited amount of time, and may differ if it is researched among different participants, sample sizes, timelines, and areas.

Independent Variables and Hypotheses

The survey was separated into two sections to measure separate independent variable groups. Dummy tables have been provided to illustrate the types of responses being measured. The first section prompts respondents to rate on a Likert scale the degree of influence initial cost, time to pay back, perceived benefits, rising costs of traditional energy sources, government incentives, perceived effectiveness, observability, complexity, suppliers' reliability, environmental responsibility, aesthetic appearance, trends toward using renewable energy sources, and social networks had on their decision to use solar power technology in their home (see Table J. 2). Responses on the scale include strong negative (1), negative (2), no effect (3), positive (4), and strong positive (5).

The second section of questions addresses demographic variables, including the level of education, current homeownership, annual household income, and monthly household energy expenses (see Table J.1). Each independent variable was categorized according to the two groups of respondents: users and nonusers. Every variable was analyzed using descriptive statistics. Then, following the model outlined in the *Theoretical Construct*, the demographic variables in the second section were examined against the attitudinal variables in the first section.

Table J.1 Attitudinal variables (five-point Likert scale)

Variable	Research	Level	Responses
Initial costs (relative advantage)	Qualitative	Ordinal	Strong negative = 1, Negative = 2, No influence = 3, Positive = 4, Strong positive = 5
Time required to pay back (relative advantage)	Qualitative	Ordinal	Strong negative = 1, Negative = 2, No influence = 3, Positive = 4, Strong positive = 5
Perceived benefits from use (relative advantage)	Qualitative	Ordinal	Strong negative = 1, Negative = 2, No influence = 3, Positive = 4, Strong positive = 5
Rising costs of traditional energy sources (relative advantage)	Qualitative	Ordinal	Strong negative = 1, Negative = 2, No influence = 3, Positive = 4, Strong positive = 5
Government incentives to offset costs (relative advantage)	Qualitative	Ordinal	Strong negative = 1, Negative = 2, No influence = 3, Positive = 4, Strong positive = 5
Perceived effectiveness of solar energy Systems (relative advantage)	Qualitative	Ordinal	Strong negative = 1, Negative = 2, No influence = 3, Positive = 4, Strong positive = 5
Observation of others in the area using solar energy (observability)	Qualitative	Ordinal	Strong negative = 1, Negative = 2, No influence = 3, Positive = 4, Strong positive = 5
How complex the technology seemed to be (complexity)	Qualitative	Ordinal	Strong negative = 1, Negative = 2, No influence = 3, Positive = 4, Strong positive = 5

The suppliers' reliability (compatibility)	Qualitative	Ordinal	Strong negative = 1, Negative = 2, No influence = 3, Positive = 4, Strong positive = 5
My environmental responsibility (compatibility)	Qualitative	Ordinal	Strong negative = 1, Negative = 2, No influence = 3, Positive = 4, Strong positive = 5
The aesthetic appearance of solar energy systems (compatibility)	Qualitative	Ordinal	Strong negative = 1, Negative = 2, No influence = 3, Positive = 4, Strong positive = 5
Trends toward using renewable energy sources (social influences)	Qualitative	Ordinal	Strong negative = 1, Negative = 2, No influence = 3, Positive = 4, Strong positive = 5
My social network (social influences)	Qualitative	Ordinal	Strong negative = 1, Negative = 2, No influence = 3, Positive = 4, Strong positive = 5

Table J.2 Demographic variables

Variable	Research	Level	Responses
Adoption of solar power system	Qualitative	Nominal	Current users = 1, Nonusers = 0
Adopter type	Qualitative	Ordinal	This year = 1, 1–5 years ago = 2 6–10 years ago = 3, 11–15 years ago = 4 16–10 years ago = 5
Education	Qualitative	Ordinal	Did not graduate high school = 0, High school graduate = 1, Some college = 2, Bachelor = 3, Master = 4, PhD = 5
Home ownership	Qualitative	Nominal	Yes = 1, No = 0
Annual household income	Quantitative	Interval	Less than $50,000 = 0, $50,000–$74,999 = 1 $75,000–$99,000 = 2, $100,000–$124,999 = 3 $125,000 or more = 4
Monthly household energy expense	Quantitative	Interval	Under $50 = 0, $50–$100=1 $101–$150 = 2, $151–$200 = 3 $201 or more = 4

Relative Advantage Variables

The following variables are being measured under the relative advantage category:

- Initial costs
- Time required to pay back
- Perceived benefits from use
- Rising costs of traditional energy sources
- Perceived effectiveness of solar energy systems

Hypotheses based on these variables are as follows:

H_1: *Every relative advantage variable is positively correlated to the dependent variable.*

Observability Variable

Effects of observability were measured by the responses to the following: Seeing others in the area using solar energy in their home.

H_2: *Observability is positively correlated to the dependent variable.*

Complexity

Effects of complexity were measured by the responses to the following: How complex the technology seemed to be

H_3: *Complexity is positively correlated to the dependent variable.*

Compatibility

Effects of compatibility were measured to reflect the compatibility factor from Rogers' Diffusion of Innovation (2003) theory, described as how technology complies with consumers' values, experiences, or needs:

- The suppliers' reliability (needs, values)
- My environmental responsibility (values)
- The aesthetic appearance of solar energy systems (values)

H_4: *Compatibility variables are positively correlated to the dependent variable.*

Social Influences

Effects of social influences were measured to reflect the *subjective norm* influence from the theory of Reasoned Action, described as the observed social pressure to act or not act on a decision (Ajzen and Fishbein 1980): Trends toward using renewable energy sources

My social network

H_5: *Social Influences are positively correlated to the dependent variable.*

Data Tests

Descriptive Statistics

The attitudinal variables being measured are related to factors described in Rogers' Diffusion of Innovations theory—Relative Advantage, observability, complexity, and compatibility—as well as social influences on a consumer's decision. These factors were chosen in order to best summarize the many possible influences that are related to each factor. Descriptive statistics were performed to summarize the average responses from participants. Chi-squared analysis was performed to determine the level of dependence between the two respondent groups: the users and non-users of domestic solar power systems, as well as the goodness of fit for each variable.

Simple Regression

According to the model that was described in the *Theoretical Construct*, this study will conduct the conceptual model as following:

The adoption rate of the solar power system = Relative advantage + Observability + Complexity + Compatibility + Social influences ($Yi = b_0 + b_1X_1 + b_2X_2 + b_3X_3 + b_4X_4 + b_5X_5$)

Yi = Adoption rate of the solar power system
X_1 = Relative advantage
X_2 = Observability
X_3 = Complexity
X_4 = Compatibility
X_5 = Social influences

Constant b_0 indicates the intercept of the regression, with all values held at zero. The coefficients of variables b_1-b_5 describe the degree of effect each factor has on the dependent variable. These coefficients were determined using multiple regression analysis to find the equation that best fits the data. Pearson correlation tests were performed to analyze the effects of the demographic data on the attitudinal responses. The same test was used to analyze the effects of attitudinal and social influence responses on the dependent variable.

Undefined Variables

In order to obtain more influences that were not included in the initial section of the survey, an open-ended question was posed in which respondents could give further insights on their decision factors:

"Please provide any other comments about factors that affected your decision to use (or not use) solar power technology for your home."

Conclusions were drawn based on results against the proposed hypotheses. The results in this study were compared against similar studies conducted in Taiwan, the Netherlands, Germany, United Kingdom, China, and Pakistan. Due to limitations of time, recommendations for additional survey respondents may be proposed to help support or refute the conclusions drawn from the preliminary data.

Example Conclusion of a Project that Contributes to Theory

A team did research on solar energy, and in particular, on feed-in-tariffs (FITs). FITs relate to an amount of money paid by the government or a utility provider for energy produced by a renewable energy source. The student team was interested in researching the influence of FITs on the adoption of solar energy and did a comparison across different nations. At the end of the study, they had the following conclusions, discussion of limitations, and directions for future research.

A powerful driver in developing the use of solar photovoltaic (PV) has been the commitment of governments. FITs have been widely used by governments as a means of stimulating solar PV growth and other renewable energy sources. FITs vary by country and are complex in nature due to the multitude of variables that can make up a FIT structure. This study examined the effects FIT policies have on the solar PV growth using data collected from 31 countries over a period of five years (2007–2011). In examining whether stronger FIT policies promoted more PV growth over poor FIT policies, this study ranked each country based on the three most prominent variables affecting the strength of FIT policies. After performing a two-sample t-test, ANOVA test, and regression analysis, the following was concluded: countries with FIT policies in place experience more solar PV growth than countries without FIT policies in place. There is a statistical difference between the means of different ranked FIT countries. The results were inconclusive in drawing the conclusion that having a higher-rated FIT policy promotes more growth. The regression performed in this study only accounts for approximately 12.8 percent of the PV growth rate; therefore, while FITs can play a role in driving solar PV growth, there are other factors that promote this growth as well.

The first limitation within our study is the time period used, spanning from 2007 to 2011. With the first national FIT established in 1990 (Fulton 2009), this study covers only a subset of the total time period representing FIT program establishments. With the continued growth of government policies supporting renewable energy, including FITs, choosing a later start date provided the use of a larger sample of countries, and therefore, better representation of overall FIT programs today. Another limitation within this study resulting from the fixed time period of 2007 to 2011 is the bias related to the growth rate of countries. This bias exists because not all countries within this study enacted FIT programs at the same time. The complexity of different FIT structures among countries creates the limitation of inconsistent variables among this dataset. Because no two FIT programs are identical, this study is unable to examine FITs using a constant set of variables among the dataset. Moreover, the payout of FITs can be variable and fluctuates year to year. This creates another limitation within this study due to the inconsistency year over year. With multiple and varying factors making up a FIT program across countries, the data is limited and inconsistent. In order to rank the countries presented in this study, only a few factors were compared. These factors were chosen based on availability of data and research supporting its importance. This creates another limitation within this study. Finally, these studies choose to exclude one data point from the Czech Republic due to an overwhelming one-year growth in PV capacity. This study believes that this data point was due to unusual circumstances that did not paint an accurate picture of the entire data within the study.

There are areas of further research that could provide important information on FITs and solar PV growth among nations. As indicated in our results, other factors influence the growth rate of solar

PV. These factors may include the solar irradiance of countries, the size and GDP of countries, the cost of electricity, renewable energy awareness among countries, and so on. A broader focused study incorporating all of the factors affecting the solar PV growth is recommended in order to better determine the role FITs play on the growth of solar PV. A second study looking at all of the variables of FIT structures could better determine which factors have the largest influence on the success of FIT programs. For example, this study could not conclude that having a higher-rated FIT program promoted more PV growth. A study may need to be done to go deeper into the factors that make up FIT structures. It could be possible, for instance, that program caps could be the biggest factor within FIT polices that affect growth. This type of study would be valuable so that governments could enact a FIT policy based on the results to promote PV growth, if that was their objective. This study may not have concluded that having a stronger FIT promote more PV growth; however, the study did find that having a strong FIT program does not necessary cause more PV growth. A further look into the factors of FIT would be very beneficial to understand how to create a FIT program that promotes growth. Third, a study could be conducted that examines the growth rate of countries immediately following FIT policy enactments to determine whether a consistent growth curve consists among varying countries.

APPENDIX L

Example Reflection on a Project that Contributes to Theory

The course theme for a research project was identified as developments for the BRIC nations. Within this theme, student teams had freedom to define their own project focus. One group decided to do research on the effects of income levels on movie consumption in the BRIC countries compared with the United States. At the end of the course, the students were asked to reflect upon the project. The student team reflection is shown as follows:

> This course has proven to be the most interesting course we have taken in the MBA program. What did we learn? The most important thing that we learned is the concept of critical thinking. No matter whether we are in class or writing a paper at home, we must always think critically, and continuously ask "why" on many different stages. Continually asking questions and carefully evaluating what constitutes sufficient, rational proof of claims helps us dig into any text as deeply as possible, and unpack every detail so as to develop a better understanding of its context. In this class, critical thinking helped us develop a deeper understanding of our research topic and perform better on our project; continuously asking questions and careful evaluations forced us to think about our project all the time. For example, at first, we decided to use GNI (gross national income) to measure personal wealth, and ticket sales in dollars to measure movie consumption. But, after we did some further research and we carefully considered the implications of these measures, we changed our variables and

chose to use disposable income to measure personal wealth and cinema attendance to measure movie consumption. GNI, we realized, is far too broad a measure to be of use in our specific context, whereas disposable income represents what people actually spend, and thus can better account for the relationship we are interested in—between an increase in personal wealth and movie consumption. In addition, we also learned that no part of the paper was perfectly finished at any moment; each section needed refinement many times, and that when we made changes in one section of our research paper, we found that many other sections we thought were nearly finished were affected, and thus needed further refinement. Whenever we discussed our research project with the professor, we got many helpful (though painfully labor-intensive) suggestions to improve our paper.

One of the most challenging parts of this project involved the ability to remain on track with the flow of development. It was extremely easy to find ourselves expanding on our topic to the point where it would not be feasible to finish within the period of a 10-week quarter. Continual focus, and a pullback to the main point, helped to keep us within the proper boundaries of this project. Each time we delved into a specific point, such as the development of our topic, the refinement of our research questions, the proper mechanisms to measure our variables, and the formation of our conceptual model, we faced the temptation to change our direction. The discovery that our topic was not as clear as needed allowed the topic to change. Discussions regarding which measurements to use as our variables opened the possibility to choose different variables. However, the choice of different variables would inevitably again change the direction of our research topic. As our topic morphed and variables changed, our conceptual model took on numerous images. The ability to remain on track during this flow of development was extremely important to the successful completion of our research project.

No part of this research process progressed smoothly, and it proved to follow the initial cycle described to us in the beginning of the quarter.[1] The writing and research process had many high and low points—there were periods where enthusiasm was high and progress seemed to be right on track, only to be followed by a sudden drop back into uncertainty. At first, we had no idea about what direction to take our project in or how to even begin to narrow down our research question. At that stage in the process, we were at a low point in the cycle. But, after many long discussions, we found our focus, established a direction, and began the work on research. At this time, we were well on our way to our first high point—we were feeling pretty good about ourselves and our project; inevitably this was followed by another plunge, and so on. During the process of developing our research project, we encountered many setbacks. These problems pushed us back into long discussions with one another and constant revisions, all of which was supported and shaped by our weekly meetings with the professor. This forced us to dig into our research as deeply as possible and to continuously work on the creative development and modification of our research paper. Constant communication and focused attention of each group member are what enabled us to get through the process.

One quarter is too short a time to do a perfect research project, and we faced many limitations. If we had the opportunity to do this research project again, we would like to include additional variables so as to make our research stronger and more comprehensive. For example, in this paper, we only used one measurement, disposable income, as an influential factor on consumer behavior. But, clearly, there are many other factors to consider; as mentioned in our paper, age, gender, family structure, social class, race, ethnicity, and geography (among others) will likely have an influence on movie consumption. Another interesting area of expansion would be on the countries involved and the amount of data used as a timeline. Five countries may not provide a large

---

[1] This was Figure 6.5

enough selection to establish a definable trend in movie consumption. When looking at emerging countries and consumer behavior within those countries, a larger population may smooth results and provide a more reliable picture. A longer period of data would also provide a better picture of trends among emerging markets.

For this course, we can provide some important recommendations for future students. First, good and ongoing communication with one's group members as well as with the professor is extremely important. Good communication can provide a clear direction on how to solve problems and allows you to solve problems by building off one another's critical perspectives. It allows all members of the group to experience the progression of learning and to benefit from the lessons of the course. Second, continual use of critical thinking is very important for this course. As aforementioned, continually asking questions helped us to think more deeply and critically about our project. Continual focus on the components of our project allowed us to pay more attention to important details and improve the quality of our paper. The last but not least recommendation to future students is to pay attention closely to the lectures within the class; we learned many things more than the title of this course suggests. The opportunity to interact with individuals of various cultures and to learn how those cultures contribute to behaviors and decisions in every day interactions will have a lasting benefit for future relationships.

References

AACSB International Accreditation Coordination Committee 2013. *AACSB Assurance of Learning Standards: An Interpretation*, revised May 3, 2013. AACSB International.

Adefolarin, O.D. 2015. *Writing a Business Report.* ASIN: B00YULNVI8.

Agile Alliance 2001. "Manifesto for Agile Software Development." Retrieved from http://agilemanifesto.org/

van Aken, J.E. 1994. "De bedrijfskunde als ontwerpwetenschap, De regulatieve en reflectieve cyclus." *Bedrijfskunde* 66, no. 1, pp. 16–26.

Allen, W. February 3, 2016. "Complicated or Complex: Knowing the Difference is Important." Retrieved from http://learningforsustainability.net/post/complicated-complex/

Alves, A.C., R.M. Sousa, S. Fernandes, E. Cardoso, M.A. Carvalho, J. Figueiredo, and R.M.S. Pereira. 2016. "Teacher's Experiences in PBL: Implications for Practice." *European Journal of Engineering Education* 41, no. 2, pp. 123–41.

Anderson, L.W., D.R. Kratwohl, P.W. Airasian, K.A. Cruikshank, R.E. Mayer, P.R. Pintrich, J. Raths, and M.C. Wittrock. 2001. *A Taxonomy for Learning, Teaching, and Assessing. A Revision of Bloom's Taxonomy of Educational Objectives,* Abridged ed. New York, NY: Longman.

Arantes do Amaral, J.A., P. Gonçalves, and A. Hess. 2015. "Creating A Project-Based Learning Environment To Improve Project Management Skills Of Graduate Students." *Journal of Problem Based Learning in Higher Education* 3, no. 2, pp. 120–30.

Arum, R., and J. Roksa. 2011. *Academically Adrift, Limited Learning On College Campuses.* Chicago: The University of Chicago Press.

Arum, R., and J. Roksa. 2013. *Aspiring Adults Adrift, Tentative Transitions of College Graduates.* Chicago: The University of Chicago Press.

Baldwin, T.T., M.D. Bedell, and J.L. Johnson. 1997. "The Social Fabric of a Team-Based M.B.A. Program: Network Effects on Student Satisfaction and Performance." *Academy of Management Journal* 40, no. 6, pp. 1369–97.

Baker, D.F. 2008. "Peer Assessment in Small Groups: a Comparison of Methods." *Journal of Management Education* 32, no. 2, pp. 183–209.

Barge, S. 2010. *Principles of Problem and Project Based Learning, The Aalborg PBL Model.* Aalborg: Aalborg University.

Barney, J.B., and T. Gorman Clifford. 2010. *What I Didn't Learn in Business School, How Strategy Works in the Real World.* Boston: Harvard Business School Press.

Bell, S. 2010. "Project-Based Learning for the 21st Century: Skills for the Future." *The Clearing House: A Journal of Educational Strategies, Issues and Ideas* 83, no. 2, pp. 39–43.

Bengtsson, L., U. Elg, and J.E. Lind. 1997. "Bridging the Transatlantic Publishing Gap: How North American Reviewers Evaluate European Idiographic Research." *Scandinavian Journal of Management* 13, no. 4, pp. 473–92.

Benstead, A.V., M. Stevenson, and L.C. Hendry. 2017. "Why and How Do Firms Reshore? A Contingency-Based Conceptual Framework." *Operations Management Research* 10, nos. 3–4, pp. 85–103.

Biggs, J. 2003. *Teaching for Quality Learning At University*, 2nd ed. Berkshire: Open University Press.

Bilgin, I., M. Kemal, Y. Karakuyu, and Y.A. Eskisehir. 2015. "The Effects of Project Based Learning on Undergraduate Students' Achievement and Self-Efficacy Beliefs Towards Science Teaching." *Eurasia Journal of Mathematics, Science & Technology Education* 11, no. 3, pp. 469–77.

Bloom, B.S., ed. 1956. *Taxonomy of Educational Objectives, the Classification of Educational Goals. Handbook 1: Cognitive Domain.* New York, NY: Longman.

Borg, M., J. Kembro, J. Notander, C. Petersson, and L. Ohlsson. 2011. "Conflict Management in Student Groups—A Teacher's Perspective in Higher Education." *Högre Utbildning* 1, no. 2, pp. 111–24.

Brookfield, S.D. 2012. *Teaching for Critical Thinking, Tools and Techniques to Help Students Question Their Assumptions.* San Francisco: Jossey-Bass.

Brynjolfsson, E., and A. McAfee. 2014. *The Second Machine Age: Work, Progress, and Prosperity in a Time of Brilliant Technologies.* New York, NY: W.W. Norton & Company.

Capsim 2015. *Teammate Monitor Analyze Train Evaluate, A Technical Synopsis of the Science Behind TeamMATE.* XXX.

Chen, G., L.M. Donahue, and R.J. Klimoski. 2004. "Training Undergraduates to Work in Organizational Teams." *Academy of Management Learning and Education* 3, no. 1, pp. 27–40.

Clark, A.C., and J.V. Ernst. 2010. "Engineering and Technical Graphics Education; Using the Revised Bloom's Taxonomy." *Journal for Geometry and Graphics* 14, no. 2, pp. 217–26.

Clark, J.L., and L.R. Clark. 2016. *How 14: A Handbook for Office Professionals*, 14th ed. Boston: Cengage Learning.

Claudio, L. 2016. *How to Write and Publish a scientific Paper: The Step-by-Step Guide.* San Juan, PR: Write Science Now Publishing Co.

Cohen, S.G., D.E. Bailey. 1997. "What Makes Teams Work: Group Effectiveness Research from the Shop Floor to the Executive Suite." *Journal of Management* 23, no. 3, pp. 239–290.

Collins, J., and J. Porras. 2008. "Organizational Vision and Visionary Organizations." *California Management Review* 50, no. 2, pp. 117–37.

Daniel, C.A. 2012. *Reader-Friendly Reports, A No-nonsense Guide to Effective Writing for MBAs, Consultants, and Other Professionals.* New York, NY: McGraw-Hill.

Davis, J.R., and T. Atkinson. May 2010. "Need speed? Slow down." *Harvard Business Review.* Retrieved from https://hbr.org/2010/05/need-speed-slow-down

De Dreu, C.K.W., and L.R. Weingart. 2003. "Task Versus Relationship Conflict, Team Performance, and Team Member Satisfaction: A Meta-analysis." *Journal of Applied Psychology* 88, no. 4, pp. 741–49.

De Graaff, E., and A. Kolmos. 2003. "Characteristics of Problem-Based Learning." *International Journal of Engineering Education* 19, no. 5, pp. 657–62.

De Graaff, E., and A. Kolmos. 2007. "History of Problem-based and Project-based Learning." In *Management of Change, Implementation of Problem-Based and Project-Based Learning in Engineering,* eds. E. de Graaff and A. Kolmos. Rotterdam: Sense Publishers.

Denzin, N.K., and Y.S. Lincoln., eds. 1994. *Handbook of Qualitative Research.* Thousand Oaks, CA: Sage Publications.

Drexler A., D. Sibbet, and R.H. Forrester. 1988. "The Team Performance Model." In *Team Building: Blueprints for Productivity and Satisfaction,* eds. W.B. Reddy and K. Jamison. Alexandria, VA: NTL Institute for Applied Behavioural Sciences.

Drucker, P. 1974. *Management: Tasks Responsibilities Practices.* London: William Heinemann Ltd.

Duarte, N. 2008. *Slide:Ology, The Art and Science of Creating Great Presentations.* Sebastopol, CA: O'Reilly Media.

Duarte, N. 2010. *Resonate, Present Visual Stories That Transform Audiences.* Hoboken, NJ: John Wiley & Sons.

Duarte, N. 2012. *HBR Guide to persuasive Presentations.* Boston: Harvard Business School Publishing Corporation.

Edmondson, A.C. 2012. *Teaming, How Organizations Learn, Innovate, and Compete in the Knowledge Economy.* San Francisco: Jossey-Bass.

Eliot, M., P. Howard, F. Nouwens, A. Stojcevski, L. Mann, J.K. Prpic, R. Gabb, S. Venkatesan, and A. Kolmos. 2012. "Developing A Conceptual Model for the Effective Assessment of Individual Student Learning in Team-Based Subjects." *Australasian Journal of Engineering Education* 18, no. 1, pp. 105–112.

Ellet, W. 2007. *The Case Study Handbook: How to Read, Discuss, and Write Persuasively About Cases.* Boston: Harvard Business School Press.

Ellington, J.K., and E.C. Dierdorff. 2014. "Individual Learning in Team Training: Self-Regulation and Team Context Effects." *Small Group Research* 45, no. 1, pp. 37–67.

Ellis, A.P.J., J.R. Hollenbeck, D.R. Ilgen, C.O. Porter, B.J. West, and H. Moon. 2003. "Team Learning: Collectively Connecting the Dots." *Journal of Applied Psychology* 88, no. 5, pp. 821–35.

Flood, T.E. 2008. *MBA Fundamentals Business Writing*. New York, NY: Kaplan Publishing.

Forrester, R., and A.B. Drexler. 1999. "A Model for Team-Based Organization Performance." *Academy of Management Executive* 13, no. 3, pp. 36–49.

Fowler, F.J., Jr. 2009. *Survey Research Methods*. Los Angeles: Sage Publications.

Fowler, F.J., Jr., and T.W. Mangione. 1990. "Standardized Survey Interviewing, Minimizing Interviewer-Related Error." Newbury Park: Sage Publications.

Frame, J.D. 2003. *Managing Projects in Organizations: How to Make the Best Use of Time, Techniques, and People*. San Francisco: Jossy-Bass.

Gardiner, L.F. 1994. *Redesigning Higher Education, Producing Dramatic Gains in Student Learning*. Report No. 7. Washington, DC: Graduate School of Education and Human Development, The George Washington University.

Garner, B.A. 2013. *HBR Guide to Better Business Writing: Engage Readers, Tighten and Brighten, Make Your Case*. Boston: Harvard Business School Publishing.

Gastel, B., and R.A. Day. 2016. *How to Write and Publish A Scientific Paper*, 8th ed. Santa Barbara: ABC-CLIO.

Glasman-Deal, H. 2012. *Science Research Writing for Non-Native Speakers of English*. London: World Scientific Publishing Co.

Graen, G.B., C. Hui, and E.A. Taylor. 2006. "Experience-Based Learning About LMX Leadership and Fairness in Project Teams: a Dyadic Directional Approach." *Academy of Management Learning and Education* 5, no. 4, pp. 448–60.

Great Schools Partnership 2015. "The Glossary of Educational Reform." Retrieved from http://edglossary.org/scaffolding/

Greenhall, M. 2010. *Report Writing Skills Training Course. How to Write A Report and Executive Summary, and Plan, Design and Present Your Report*. Lancashire: University of Learning Ltd.

de Groot, A.D. 1969. *Methodology: Foundations of Inference and Research in the Behavioral Sciences*. Belgium: Mouton & Co.

Guba, E.G., and Y.S. Lincoln. 1994. "Competing Paradigms in Qualitative Research." In *Handbook of Qualitative Research*, eds. N.K. Denzin and Y.S. Lincoln, 105–17. Thousand Oaks, CA: Sage Publications.

Gummesson, E. 1991. *Qualitative Methods in Management Research*, Revised ed. Newbury Park: Sage Publications.

Gustavii, B. 2008. *How to Write and Illustrate A Scientific Paper*, 2nd ed. Cambridge: Cambridge University Press.

Haidet, P., K. Kubitz, and W.T. McCormack. 2014. "Analysis of the Team-Based Learning Literature: TBL Comes of Age." *Journal on Excellence in College Teaching* 25, nos. 3–4, pp. 303–33.

Hanna, W. 2007. "The New Bloom's Taxonomy: Implications for Music Education." *Arts Education Policy Review* 108, no. 4, pp. 7–16.

Education, Arts Education Policy Review, Harvard Business Review Staff. November 3, 2016. "The Four Phases of Project Management." *Harvard Business Review* 108, no. 4, pp. 7–16. Retrieved from https://hbr.org/2016/11/the-four-phases-of-project-management

Herman, B., and J.M. Siegelaub. 2009. "Is This Really Worth the Effort? The need for a Business Case." Paper presented at PMI® Global Congress 2009—North America, Orlando, FL. Newtown Square, PA: Project Management Institute.

Hmelo-Silver, C.E. September, 2004. "Problem-Based Learning: What and How Do Students Learn?" *Educational Psychology Review* 16, no. 3, pp. 235–66.

Hoff, R. 1992. *I Can See You Naked*. Kansas City, MO: Universal Press Syndicate Company.

Holden, G. 2011. *Business Reports for Busy People, Timesaving, Ready-to-Use Reports for Any Occasion*. Pompton Plains: The Career Press.

International Institute of Business Analysis 2015. *BABOK: A Guide to the Business Analysis Body of Knowledge V3*. Toronto, Canada: International Institute of Business Analysis.

Janesick, V.J. 1994. "The Dance of Qualitative Research Design." In *Handbook of Qualitative Research*, eds. N.K. Denzin and Y.S. Lincoln, 209–19. Thousand Oaks, CA: Sage Publications.

Karia, A. 2015. *How to Design TED Worthy Presentation Slides*. No publisher.

Lester, J.D., and J.D. Lester, Jr. 2015. *Writing Research Papers. A Complete Guide*. Pearson.

Kolmos, A. 1996. "Reflections on Project Work and Problem-Based Learning." *European Journal of Engineering Education* 21, no. 2, pp. 141–48.

Kozlowski, S.W.J., and D.R. Ilgen. 2006. "Enhancing the Effectiveness of Work Groups and Teams." *Psychological Science in the Public Interest* 7, no. 3, pp. 77–124.

Kratwohl, D.R. 2002. "A Revision of Bloom's Taxonomy: An Overview." *Theory into Practice* 41, no. 4, pp. 212–18.

Larmer, J., J. Mergendoller, and S. Boss. 2015. *Setting the Standard for Project Based Learning: A Proven Approach to Rigorous Classroom Instruction*. Alexandria, VA: ASCD.

Lee, H.J., and C. Lim. 2012. "Peer Evaluation in Blended Team Project-Based Learning: What Do Students Find Important?" *Educational Technology and Society* 15, no. 4, pp. 214–24.

Louie, K. 2005. "How Scrum Works." *Scrum Alliance*. Retrieved from https://scrumalliance.org/community/articles/2005/september/how-scrum-works

Magretta, J. 2012. *Understanding Michael Porter, The Essential Guide to Competition and Strategy.* Boston: Harvard Business Review Press.

Mayer, R.E. 2002. "Rote Versus Meaningful Learning." *Theory in Practice* 41, no. 4, pp. 226–32.

McCorkle, D.E., J. Reardon, J.F. Alexander, N.D. Kling, R.C. Harris, and R.V. Iyer. 1999. "Undergraduate Marketing Students, Group Projects, and Teamwork: the Good, the Bad, and the Ugly?" *Journal of Marketing Education* 21, no. 2, pp. 106–17.

McManus, D.A. Novermber, 2001. "The Two Paradigms of Education and the Peer Review of Teaching." *Journal of Geoscience Education* 49, no. 5, pp. 423–34.

Michaelsen, L.K., N. Davidson, and C.H. Major. 2014. "Team-Based Learning Practices and Principles in Comparison with Cooperative Learning and Problem-Based Learning." *Journal in Excellence in College Teaching* 25, nos. 3–4, pp. 57–84.

Mooney, C.G. 2000. *Theories of Childhood: An Introduction to Dewey, Montessori, Erickson, Piaget and Vygotsky.* St. Paul: Redleaf Press.

Morris, P. 1994. *The Management of Projects.* London: Thomas Telford.

Norad 1999. *Logical Framework Approach: Handbook for Objectives-Oriented Planning.* Oslo, Norway: Norwegian Agency for Development Cooperation (Norad).

Oakley, B., R.M. Felder, R. Brent, and I. Elhajj. 2004. "Turning Student Groups into Effective Teams." *Journal of student centered learning* 2, no. 1, pp. 9–34.

Pentland, A.S. 2012. "The New Science of Building Great Teams." *Harvard Business Review* April, pp. 60–70.

Pickard, M.J. 2007. "The New Bloom's Taxonomy, An Overview for Family and Consumer Sciences." *Journal of Family and Consumer Sciences Education* 25, no. 1, pp. 45–55.

Platts, K.W., and N. Song. 2010. "Overseas Sourcing Decisions—The Total Cost of Sourcing from China." *Supply Chain Management: An International Journal* 15, no. 4, pp. 320–31.

Porter, M.E. 1980. *Competitive Strategy.* New York, NY: The Free Press.

Porter, M.E. 1990. *The Competitive Advantage of Nations.* New York, NY: The Free Press.

Prince, M.J., and R.M. Felder. 2006. "Inductive Teaching and Learning Methods: Definitions, Comparisons, and Research Bases." *Journal of Engineering Education* April, pp. 123–38.

Project Management Institute 2006. *Practice Standard for Work Breakdown Structures*, 2nd ed. Newtown Square, PA: Project Management Institute.

Project Management Institute 2013. *A Guide to the Project Management Body of Knowledge*, 5th ed. Newtown Square: Project Management Institute Inc.

Project Management Institute 2017a. *A Guide to the Project Management Body of Knowledge (PMBOK Guide)*, 6th ed. Newtown Square, PA: Project Management Institute.

Project Management Institute 2017b. *Agile Practice Guide*. Newtown Square, PA: Project Management Institute.

Project Management Institute Educational Foundation 2016. *Project Management for Career and Technical Education: Marketing Projects*. Newtown Square, PA: Project Management Institute Educational Foundation.

Ramsden, P. 2003, *Learning to Teach in Higher Education,* 2nd ed. London: RouthledgeFalmer.

Ricardo, D. 1996. *Principles of Political Economy and Taxation*. Originally published 1911. Amherst: Prometheus Books.

Salas, E., D.E. Sims, and C.S. Burke. 2005. "Is there a "Big Five" in Teamwork?" *Small Group Research* 36, no. 5, pp. 555–99.

Samuelowics, K., and J.D. Bain. April 2001. "Revisiting Academics' Beliefs about Teaching and Learning." *Higher Education* 41, no. 3, pp. 299–325.

Savery, J.R. 2015. "Overview of Problem-Based Learning: Definitions and Distinctions." In *Essential Readings in Problem-Based Learning: Exploring and Extending the Legacy of Howard S. Barrows,* eds. P.A. Ertmer, C. Hmelo-Silver, A. Walker, and H. Leary. West Lafayette, IN: Purdue University Press.

Schwaber, K. 2009. *Agile Project Management with Scrum*. Redmond, WA: Microsoft Press.

Schwaber, K., and J. Sutherland. November, 2017. "The Scrum Guide, the Definitive Guide to Scrum: The Rules of the Game." Retrieved from http://scrumguides.org/docs/scrumguide/v2017/2017-Scrum-Guide-US.pdf#zoom=100

Schwandt, T.A. 1994. "Constructivist, Interpretivist Approaches to Human Inquiry." In *Handbook of Qualitative Research*, eds. N.K. Denzin and Y.S. Lincoln, 118–37. Thousand Oaks, CA: Sage Publications.

Sibbet, D. 2003. *Principles of Facilitation, The Purpose and Potential of Leading Group Process*. San Francisco: The Grove Consultants International.

Snyder, C.S. 2013. *A Project Manager's Book of Forms,* 2nd ed. Hoboken, NJ: John Wiley & Sons.

Stacey, R. 1996. *Complexity and Creativity in Organizations*. Oakland, CA: Berrett-Koehler Publishers.

Stegeager, N., A.O. Thomassen, and E. Laursen. 2013. "Problem Based Learning in Continuing Education—Challenges and Opportunities." *Journal of Problem Based Learning in Higher Education* 1, no. 2, pp. 151–57.

Stentoft, D., M. Duroux, T. Fink, and J. Emmersen. 2014. "From Cases to Projects in Problem-Based Medical Education." *Journal of Problem Based Learning in Higher Education* 2, no. 1, pp. 45–62.

Stewart, G.L. 2006. "A Meta-Analytic Review of Relationships Between Team Design Features and Team Performance." *Journal of Management* 32, no. 1, pp. 29–55.

van Strien, P.J. 1986. *Praktijk Als Wetenschap; Methodologie Van Het Sociaal-Wetenschappelijk Handelen.* Assen, the Netherlands: Van Gorcum.

Thomas, J.W. 2010. "A Review of Research On Project-Based Learning." http://autodesk.com/foundation (accessed April 8, 2017).

Trent, R.J., and R.M. Monczka. 2003. "Understanding Integrated Global Sourcing." *International Journal of Physical Distribution and Logistics Management* 33, no. 7, pp. 607–29.

Trilling, B., and W. Ginevri. 2017. *Project Management for Education: The Bridge to 21st Century learning.* Newtown Square, PA: Project Management Institute.

Tuckman, B.W. 1965. "Developmental Sequence in Small Groups." *Psychological Bulletin* 63, no. 6, pp. 384–99.

van Rooij, S.W. 2009. "Scaffolding Project-based Learning with the Project Management Body of Knowledge (PMBOK)." *Computers & Education* 52, pp. 210–19.

Verschuren, P., and H. Doorewaard. 1999. *Designing a Research Project.* Utrecht, the Netherlands: Lemma.

Wallace, M.L., J.D. Walker, A.M. Braseby, and M.S. Sweet. 2014. "Now, What Happens During Class? Using Team-based Learning to Optimize the Role of Expertise Within the Flipped Classroom." *Journal on Excellence in College Teaching* 25, nos. 3 and 4, pp. 253–73.

Wysocki, R. 2014. *Effective Project Management: Traditional, Agile, Extreme,* 7th ed. Indianapolis, IN: John Wiley & Sons, Inc.

Zikmund, W.G., B.J. Babin, J.C. Carro, and M. Griffin. 2012. *Business Research Methods,* 9th ed. Mason, OH: South-Western, Cengage Learning.

About the Authors

Harm-Jan Steenhuis is a Professor of Management, International Business in the College of Business at Hawai'i Pacific University. He previously worked at Eastern Washington University, North Carolina State University, and the University of Twente at Enschede, the Netherlands. He received his MSc in Industrial Engineering and Management and his PhD in International Technology Transfer from the University of Twente at Enschede, The Netherlands. He has taught project-based learning oriented courses with many different types of projects.

Lawrence Rowland is an associate professor of Information Systems in the College of Business at Hawaii Pacific University. He previously founded and ran Applied Analysis Inc., in Honolulu. Lawrence obtained his Ed.D. from the University of Southern California, where he also received a MS in Systems Management. He also obtained a MS in Agricultural and Resource Economics from the University of Hawaii, Manoa. Larry founded and is currently the College Relations director for the Project Management Institute Honolulu Hawaii Chapter. Larry has taught project management at HPU for over twenty years and overseen hundreds of student/community projects.

Index